SAVE
THE PLANET

SAVE
THE PLANET

AN AMAZONIAN TRIBAL LEADER FIGHTS
FOR HIS PEOPLE, THE RAINFOREST,
AND THE EARTH

ALMIR NARAYAMOGA SURUÍ
AND CORINE SOMBRUN

schaffner
press

To my parents, Marimop and Weytam,
and my wives, Adlanes and Ivaneide,
to my children, Oyexiener, Oyexepo, Walelasoepilemān,
Walelasoetxeiged and Walelasoekim,
and the great Amazon forest, our Mother

A.N.S.

To Brigitte, to la Yourte, and to Jules

C.S.

"The indigenous way is so surprising because
it is not used to produce, but to live"
—**BETTY MINDLIN, anthropologist and author, *Wild Notes***

"The forest that I have come to know will never let us die of hunger."
—**CÂNDIDO RONDON, early Brazilian explorer**

"The lands of the Whites are contaminated, poisoned.
They will never know what the shamans know. All they think of ceaselessly
are their possessions, as if these were their lovers . . ."
—**DAVI YANOMAMI, Yanomami shaman
and spokesperson for the Yanomami tribe**

CONTENTS

Venezuela

Guyana

Colombia

Surinam

French Guyana

Ecuador

Amazon

Manaus

Belém

Brazil

Peru

Rondônia

Mato Grosso

Bolivia

Brasilia

Salvador

Paraguay

São Paulo

Chile

Rio de Janeiro

Argentina

Uruguay

·········· Boundaries of Brazilian State
1000 km

Towards Manaus

Amazon

Porto Velho

BR-364

Rondônia

Suruí Territory

Mato Grosso

Ji-Paraná

Presidente Médici

Lapetanha

Cacoal

Espigão d'Oeste

BOLIVIA

Vilhena

200 km

Towards Caceres

FOREWORD

BY CORINE SOMBRUN

Today, Brazil encompasses 654 indigenous territories that make up 15% of its total surface area. Within these territories is the one belonging to the *Paiter Suruí,* whose ancestral name is *Paiter,* meaning "the true people, we ourselves[1]." The first white contact with this long-isolated Amazonian people occurred with representatives of Brazilian authorities in 1969. In 1971 only 204 Suruí out of a population of 5,000 had survived the epidemics that were prompted by that first contact. Their land is situated in the State of Rondônia in northwestern Brazil, north of the city of Cacoal. Today, their reserve, called Terra Indígena Sete de Setembro (Seventh of September Reserve) stretches across 247,870 hectares (957 square miles), twice the surface area of New York City and twenty times the surface area of Paris.

Almir Narayamoga Suruí is their charismatic and visionary leader. "Now we are fourteen hundred," he says, "and we have survived successfully. But our priority is to protect the rainforest and to warn the rest of humanity about the necessity of preserving this vital lung, this source of oxygen, for future generations." In a half-century, the Brazilian Amazon rainforest population has grown from 6 to 25 million inhabitants, bringing about a massive reduction of forest surface area in favor of agriculture and timber production. The state of Rondônia is one of the hardest-hit by deforestation and has suffered a loss of 40% of its primary forest. On a broader scale, close to one fifth of the Amazon rainforest has disappeared since 1970 and about 17% of it (60 million hectares, nearly 232,000 square miles, the surface area of France or Texas), has been

1: *Translation taken from Enciclopédia dos Povos Indígenas no Brasil - Instituto Socioambiental (https://pib.socioambiental.org/en/povo/surui-paiter/print)*

repurposed in the last thirty years, according to 2008 data from the National Institute for Space Research in Brazil (IPNE).

Almir Narayamoga Suruí decided to "do his part" to fight this ecological catastrophe and to help protect the planet by putting in place a 50-year plan for reforestation and the sustainable management of the rainforest's resources. He is also the one at the heart of the Suruí Forest Carbon Project, a pioneering project that has made the Suruí the first indigenous group to generate carbon credits to finance the preservation of their rainforest.

"In August 2013," says Almir Suruí, "the Brazilian beauty products giant Natura Cosméticos bought 120,000 tons of carbon compensation from us (Verified Carbon Standard). This transaction was the first of its kind and I know that it will be of interest not only to other tribes in the Amazon rainforest, but also to companies and institutions that want to stay in compliance with their visions of and goals for environmental responsibility. This model would allow tribes to be remunerated for preserving, reforesting, and maintaining the rainforest."

Almir Narayamoga Suruí was awarded the Human Rights Prize in 2008 in Geneva by the International Society for Human Rights, and was named one of the 100 most influential people in Brazil by Época magazine in 2009. In 2013, Brazilian President Dilma Rousseff awarded him the Human Rights Award. Today, he is a liaison between his people and the government, but his struggle against deforestation has made him the enemy of many timber poachers. Several bounties and contracts have been taken out against him, and in July of 2012, the government assigned him two permanent body guards from the federal police special forces. International businesses and organizations such as Google Earth, ACT, Kanindé, USAID, Forest Trends, IDESAM[2], Funbio[3] and Aquaverde were moved by the courage of Almir Narayamoga Suruí and his people and have supported them both financially and logistically.

I had the opportunity to meet Almir Narayamoga Suruí in February of 2011 when I was working on a playwriting project started by the actress Agnès Soral. Soral is a sponsor and supporter of the Aquaverde organization, along with its president Thomas Pizer. In 2008 when Suruí members visited the Avignon Theater Festival, chief Almir

2: *Institute for the Conservation and Sustainable Development of the Amazon*
3: *Brazilian Biodiversity Fund*

asked Soral and Pizer to help train and educate his people in the performing arts and entertainment, "a platform that the Indians could use to spread their ecological message throughout the world in a more playful way."

That was how in 2011 I was able to join the incredible adventure of accompanying Agnès Soral and Thomas Pizer into the Amazon rainforest. The idea for this book was born after we met with Almir Narayamoga Suruí: I would tell the story of his people from the time of the first official white contact as well as the extraordinary human drama that has made him a leader in the fight against the ecologically catastrophic deforestation of the Amazon.

"The Amazon rainforest stretches across nearly 60 million square kilometers (3.7 million square miles) and over nine countries (Brazil, Bolivia, Peru, Ecuador, Colombia, Venezuela, Guyana, Suriname and French Guiana)," Almir Narayamoga Suruí explains. "It is the largest reservoir of biodiversity in the world and the largest tropical rainforest, home to nearly 390 billion trees of approximately 16,000 different species."

This book, envisioned as a way of recording his ideological legacy, is the first written account of Almir Suruí's story. He does not simply warn the rest of the world against the serious risks of irresponsible behavior. Rather, he demonstrates that preserving the rainforest can generate more revenue than what can be generated by destroying it, and he provides us concrete solutions for saving the biodiversity of our planet.

Corine Sombrun

PROLOGUE

November 6, 2013

8:31am

Seventh of September Indigenous Reserve

"It's time," my body guard Sergente, said readjusting the assault rifle slung over his shoulder.

I looked one last time at the tombstone. My father's soul had gone off towards the horizon to join the *Gorakoy*, or the "kingdom of the waters" situated to the west, and all of a sudden, I was scared of no longer having enough time to tell you that if you do not talk to the trees, they will disappear.

The clicking of Sergente's MD97 brought me back to the moment. "Even at 89, your father didn't have a single gray hair!" he said, apologizing for interrupting me in thought. I smiled sadly.

"Our people, the *Paiter Suruí* don't go gray. If I live long enough, my hair will have stayed as black as it is now. Did you know that laboratories sold our blood samples under the guise of vaccinating us in order to identify the gene related to keeping our hair from turning gray—a visible sign of eternal youth?"

"Yes, I read about it online. But we have to get going now . . ."

I sighed and turned one last time to address my father. "Rest in peace in this forest that you loved so much, Marimop. The forest's ancestral spirits will continue to protect you." Our people do not cut down trees or overhunt game to ensure that we don't disturb them. These spirits watch over us and must be respected, "as much as the light of day," my father would say when I was very little. "The daylight is a living thing that you can only mention at night, at very specific times."

My puzzled expression had urged him on. The tattoo running the length of his smile

stretched slightly. "Because the daylight could get upset!"

Without speaking its name, I watched the daylight tint the sky in pinkish hues. Then I walked away into the rustling of the *babaçu* leaves. Sergente positioned himself behind me, one hand on the stock of his gun. I told him that the only thing we had to fear right now was rain. He looked up, surprised, at the treetops of the *pacohb* where I was looking.

"How do you know?"

"The sound of the forest is different—as though she is getting ready. Do you have an umbrella?"

"No, the only thing I have to protect that head of yours is an assault rifle!"
I couldn't help but laugh. The timber poachers had promised $100,000 to whomever could bring them my head. Quite a sum. They are upset because I spoke out against their greediness and found a way to make a profit off the Amazon rainforest without destroying it—certainly enough to upset them.

"So," Sergente began cautiously, "in 2000 I was sent to Bahia for the commemoration of the 500th anniversary of the discovery of Brazil . . ."

"I was there as well!"

"Well, I didn't know you at the time, but I was in charge of 'targeting' indigenous leaders during the protests . . . Do you see what I'm getting at?"

I nodded.

"If I would have known that you were one of them," he continued, "I have to admit that I would have followed my orders." He looked at me sadly. "Do you hold that against me?"

"None of that had anything to do with you. It's simply politics. And now you've been assigned to protect me!"

Sergente grinned.

"I have to admit something else. With everything that people say about natives, I was scared to death when they told me was I was being assigned to an indigenous leader. I nearly begged them to give me another assignment!"

I burst out laughing. "And now?"

Sergente adjusted his purple cap.

"Well, when my boss told me I was finally going to be able to switch assignments, I begged him to let me stay on with you." He looked down shyly at his shoes. "I have actually never been treated with as much respect before you," he added. "It's important

for me to tell you that it's been an honor to be assigned to protect you."

I looked down in turn.

"Thank you for those words, Sergente. That means a lot to me. Now it's my turn—can I tell you something?"

He waited. I was holding the tiny USB drive that I always kept in my pocket. It contained the history of my people since the first official contact with whites in 1969—a life's work in a PDF: the sustainable management plan for our giant rainforest's resources for the next fifty years.

"Will you give this to my children, if . . ."

He held out his hand then pulled it back. He looked at me.

"Almir, is this your wi—" He cleared his throat.

"I don't know if what is on this will awaken the consciences of those who destroy the rainforest," I said reassuringly, "but at least they will know that our people did our part, and that it's very urgent that they do theirs."

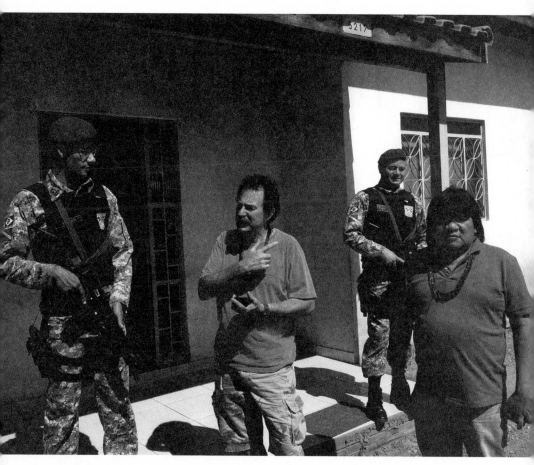

In response to the death threats from the madeireiros, the Brazilian government provided Chief Almir with body guards from the special forces of the Brazilian federal police for protection.

© T. Pizer, Aquaverde, 2012

1975. Yerah Suruí wearing traditional jewelry.
(Associação Metareilá Suruí)

PART I

When the world was created, God came to visit us. Because he was very ugly, we did not recognize him and we did not treat him well. When he asked to lie down and rest, we gave him our worst hammock. When he wanted to drink chicha, we served it to him in the bowl for the dog. So, he left. He came back in the form of a very handsome man who was playing the flute. We still did not recognize him, but because he was very handsome, and we suggested that he lie down and rest in our best hammock. "No, no," he said, "the last time you gave me the worst one. This one will be enough." To drink the chicha we gave him the best bowl we had. "No, no," he said again, "I'll drink from the bowl for the dogs." But when it was time to leave he took a stone and threw it on the big maloca where we were all gathered. It was oval shaped and had a roof and walls of braided straw, but it was transformed instantly into stone and it became impossible for us to get out. We were desperate and we asked the woodpecker to make a hole with his beak. He could not. We asked the macaw to make a hole with his beak. He could not. It was finally the regeti that saved us. Although the bird is very small, his spirit is very big. He only made a tiny hole, but four among us were able to get out. Those were the ancestors of our people, the Paiter Suruí.

CONTACT

My name is Almir Narayamoga Suruí and this is my legacy.
I was born on August 19, 1974 in the State of Rondônia, on the 7ᵗʰ of September Indigenous
Reserve. At the age of 36, I was elected the leader of the Paiter Suruí people. As you know,
my whole life has been dedicated to the struggle to help my people survive. And to help the
Amazon rainforest survive.
Now I am in my forties.
I have two wives.
I have my six children.
And two body guards.

I must begin by saying that everything started with the BR-364, the dirt road built by the whites at the beginning of the 1960s to reach the unexplored land of the northwest Brazilian Amazon. The 5,000 people that made up the Paiter Suruí lived on a territory twenty times the size of New York City, about 12,500 square miles. Our ancestors settled here at some point during the 19th century in order to flee the advancing settlers. But from the 1900s on, the opening of the Madeira-Mamoré railroad and the installation of the first telegraph line in the Amazon endangered our isolation. One can easily imagine reasons why this was the case, but to help you understand what was at stake, I feel it is important to take the time to explain a few key moments in this process.

First of all, the telegraph line. Colonel Cândido Rondon led the project. The line had to traverse the 906 miles of jungle connecting Cuiabá, the administrative center of the neighboring state of Mato Grosso, to Porto Velho, the administrative center of Rondônia. Despite the help of the Bororo people in the south, with whom Colonel Rondon maintained very good relations, it took four years for this project to be accomplished. The

telegraph line had to go around the Pantanal, the swampiest wetlands in the world, and reach the city of Corumba on the Paraguay River. I admit this was a tremendous feat, but it triggered the first migration wave which consisted mainly of *seringueiros*, tappers of rubber trees, drawn there by the rubber boom at the end of the 19ᵗʰ century.

This wave might not have been enough to end our isolation if not for another "rubber fever," in the 1940s, as well as the simultaneous discovery of mines of cassiterite (a tin oxide used in electronics). This provoked an increase in the population of more than 50%. Inevitably, this caused numerous conflicts with the natives. Trying to avoid all contact with these "invaders," our people decided to leave their villages and take refuge even further into the interior of the region, which was at that time called Guaporé. We live there still, but in 1946 the region's name was changed to the State of Rondônia. As you may have guessed, the name pays homage to Cândido Rondon. This change was justified by his exceptional accomplishments.

Rondon led the installation of more than 6,000 km (906 miles) of telegraph line in the jungles of Brazil and had one of his toes devoured by piranhas in the process. He led several explorations, one of which was a scientific expedition with Theodore Roosevelt on the Rio da Dúvida (the River of Doubt). In 1910, Rondon was the military engineer behind the creation of the Serviço de Proteção ao Índio (the Indian Protection Service, or SPI), which was a major advancement in the struggle for indigenous rights. But I need to get to the 1960s, which marked a pivotal moment in our tribe's history.

* * *

Rondônia's border location, as well as the pressure of the neighboring Peruvians and Bolivians (who were very numerous compared to the 70,000 Brazilians of the region), were incentives for colonization projects, one of which was the construction of roads. What drove the construction of the BR-364 road at the end of the 1950s was the Kubitschek government's desire to connect the new capital, Brasilia, to the other main cities of the country, and then to connect central Brazil to the rest of Latin America. This is how in 1964, the path to the segment connecting Cuiabá to Porto Velho (in addition to intensive agricultural development) put a definitive end to our seclusion.

At that time, we were not officially in contact with the whites and we were called

Paiter, "the true people, we ourselves" because our archery skills were so good that we did not need to put poison on our arrows to kill our targets. My father, your grand-father, also told us that our people tried to avoid depleting the rainforest by taking only the game, fruit, *gongo* (larva of the coconut borer found in the fruit of the *babaçu* palm) and honey that they needed. In order to not exhaust the land, we cultivated and regularly rotated plots of corn, manioc, yams, beans, rice, bananas, peanuts, papayas, cotton and tobacco.

We also shared social rules that were well-defined. In addition to the shared value of helping each other, the men and women planted and fished together. But it was up to the men to make the bows, the arrows and the *tembetá,* which are the *jatobá*—ornaments of polished resin—placed in the inside of the lower lip of each of the members of our tribe. Each man was also obligated to offer several days' work in the fields of any family member that did not live in his house. Additionally, men had to hunt and clear plots of land to be used for farming. The women were responsible for taking care of the children, preparing meals, weaving, and harvesting. They were also our artisans, making crafts such as ceramic pots, baskets, belts and necklaces.

Any economic activity was organized primarily around family groups, whereas community life was separated into two halves. One half was connected to the forest (the *metare* group, responsible more specifically for crafts, hunting, fishing and gathering) and the other to the plots of land (the *iwai* group, responsible for farming). But each half switched roles according to very specific cycles throughout the year. This division between tribal members working in the forest and in the fields provided the basis for our annual calendar. This calendar determined the important moments of our social world, including food production, festivals and rituals. During the dry season from May to October, the half assigned to the forest would camp at a small area (*metareilá)* cleared about 500 meters (546 yards) from the village. This space was off-limits to the other half.

Our tribe was equally divided into several clans. There were as many as ten clans before but there are only four left, as you know, called *Kaban, Gamir, Makor,* and *Gameb.* Like my father, I am a part of the *Gameb* clan, named for the most fearsome black hornet of the rainforest. This name belongs to warriors, whose role has always been to protect our people from the four other tribes of the region: the Zoró, who live to the north of our territory, the Cinta-Larga to the east between Jurena and Roosevelt, the Gavião to

the northwest and the Arara to the west of the Zoró territory. With just a few slight differences, we all speak a common language that is in the Tupi language family in the Monde branch. We manage to understand one another, but we estimate that there are 170 indigenous dialects in Brazil, mostly variations of the Tupi, Jê, Aruak, Carib and Panoan language families.

Let me come back to that morning in 1969 that was going to mark the end of our seclusion. Marimop and a few of his *Gameb* brothers had left on a scouting mission to warn of an attack of the Zoró Indians, who we call our "best enemies." Our warriors reached the summit of the highest hill of our land when in the distance, in the valley, they saw trees falling, swallowed by the mouth of an enormous snake with a yellow head. They calmly observed the animal, thinking that it would eventually eat its fill. But nothing seemed to be able to stop it. Day after day, this glutton sunk his teeth into the hévéas, the *babaçù*, the *tucumà, the copaïba, the pacohb,* the fig trees, opening and emptying the rainforest as none of their machetes had ever done before. When the creature was on the verge of entering into their territory, leaving a single furrow of red earth in its path, they decided it was time to stop it. It was then that they discovered that the white man was commanding it. Their elders had mentioned this to my grandfather and his group, but it was the first time that they had seen it for themselves. Despite the terrible scene before them, they decided to take up their role as warriors and go to face the white men and ask them to stop the animal. The leader of the white men made it clear that it was a machine, a "bulldozer," and that it was going to continue to swallow the forest.

The conflict began then and there.

We had been five thousand before this first contact. Five thousand, do you realize? Many of our warriors were killed. Many whites were killed. And the more the whites killed our people, the more of our people killed the whites. So, a man was designated to establish peaceful contact with our tribe since, according to his bosses, we were living dangerously close to the path of the BR-364 and we were in the way of its completion.

This man, Francisco Meireles, was a *sertanista*, a name given to the bureaucrats of the department that Cândido Rondon started, the SPI. These *sertanistas* were responsible for establishing contact with secluded tribes, and were generally experts in indigenous cultures. This was not the first mission of Francisco Meireles. He had been credited

with successfully establishing contact with the Xavante to the east of the neighboring state of Mato Grosso in the 1940s, and then with the Pakaá Nova tribe near the upper Madeira in 1960. It was likely thanks to him that we are named Suruí, which meant "enemy" in the language of the people that had been his guides.

Considering himself too old, in 1969, Francisco Meireles left the mission of establishing contact with tribes in the hands of his son Apoena, who had been raised after his mother's death by a woman from the Xavante tribe. The process was always the same, you see: delaying first contact until it was deemed urgent and then moving forward to establish contact in the approach phase called "the attraction." This consisted of adopting a friendly behavior with the Indians, much different from how the settlers or prospectors typically behaved, and then giving gifts that were supposed to convince the tribes to come to the table and establish communication. Once this was accomplished, the Indians were pacified as well as trained and educated in order for them to "pass from acculturation to assimilation," to use the words of the SPI.

For nine months Apoena Meireles left mirrors, pans, knives and scissors in a spot that was highly frequented by our tribe, next to the village of Riozinho. Finally, one day, a group of warriors armed with bows and arrows came to meet Meireles. He gave them two machetes and he was offered fish in return. At the second meeting, Meireles showed up nearly completely naked to show that he was not armed. He gave them more gifts and when our people accepted them, he brought more. After four or five visits, our leaders decided to accept official contact and negotiate. My father, Marimop, however, was opposed to it. He was a respected warrior and had won numerous battles against the Zoró. He had warned the tribe that these *iaraei*, these whites, did not know the rainforest and that they would not respect it, just as they had demonstrated with their bulldozer. Despite this, the majority still rallied behind the leaders' decision, arguing that they were the first foreigners not intending to massacre our people. Additionally, they felt that if we didn't make peace with these people, we would inevitably be annihilated. But wasn't the example of the Cinta-Larga in 1963 still in everyone's memory?

At that time, our neighbors still had not been officially contacted. This would happen later in 1968, but before then they did what all the other tribes had done: they defended their land against the invasion of the gold seekers, settlers, and those who came to log their precious wood, and other mining companies. Exasperated by these conflicts, the

foreman of the Arrudae Junqueira, a large rubber cultivation company, had simply decided to exterminate their tribe. Denounced later by a former inspector of the SPI of the city of Cuiabá, the foreman had rented a small Cessna plane to fly over a village in Cinta-Larga. Having taken care to choose the day that they were celebrating their yearly festivities, he flew over once and dropped packages of sugar. At first the Cinta-Larga were afraid but they quickly realized that it was food, and all gathered around to collect the packages. But they had barely opened them when the Cessna flew over once more and dropped sticks of dynamite. This attack was followed by a land raid on other villages. The testimonies recorded by a missionary and given to the SPI spoke of a veritable manhunt during which children were beheaded and women were raped. One of them was found hooked to a tree, still alive, but sliced open from pelvis to chin with a machete.

So yes, because they were asking courteously for once, our people preferred to establish peaceful contact with Apoena Meireles's team. Unfortunately, they did not suspect that this would lead to the near-elimination of our people.

First, two terrible epidemics—the flu and measles—hit our people. These were followed by a third in which the first symptoms manifested with a hoarse cough, expectorations, and a persistent fever that was fatal in less than two months. The local medical teams had no idea how to prevent and treat this sickness which was later identified as blastomycosis.

Doctor Chiappino, a French doctor, visited shortly after this contact with the whites. He was dismayed at the way in which the FUNAI (Fundação Nacional do Indio) was handling the problem. The FUNAI had replaced the SPI (Indian Protection Service) in 1967. This change was driven by some events that were so serious that I will take the time to explain them here.

As I mentioned, the SPI was created on September 7, 1910 to handle relations between the indigenous tribes and the European immigrants. The SPI was the fruit of the labor of a small group of liberal activists inspired by Cândido Rondon who was its first director. The mission of this new organization was "to provide protection and assistance to the Indians of Brazil, to secure their way of life, their freedom and their land, to defend them from annihilation, to spare them from exploitation and oppression, and to protect them from poverty." The SPI also had orders to not attempt any conversion to Catholicism or any other religion. It had thus become a secular department of the

government. I must say that after four centuries of conflict, brutality, and exploitation, the creation of this new department inspired a huge wave of hope among the Indians. Would we at last be respected and treated with decency?

Even though at first the SPI's mission was upheld, it quickly became difficult to control the agents sent into the territories that were very far removed from the central management. A local outpost was directed either by a salaried agent of the SPI or by an agent *delegado* who was not paid but who had to be able to justify his personal expenses. This inevitably led to some agents taking advantage of their local power in order to make money off of the indigenous land. They would call this "Indian payout," and it quickly became a common practice for the SPI agents to turn a blind eye to it all: the theft of indigenous land as well as the massacre of tribes who defended themselves against the loggers, prospectors, speculators and many explorers drawn by the extraordinary potential of these unexplored lands. Francisco Meireles denounced several expeditions mounted in retaliation against tribes, one of which was led by rubber tappers in 1952 against a village of Oroin Indians. He said it was known that they ripped out the eyes of Indian children before leaving them in the forest. This kind of barbarism did not help the efforts for peaceful negotiation led by Meireles in the name of the SPI. What's more, on most occasions the criminals remained unpunished. In 1967, the Minister of the Interior, General Afonso Augusto de Albuquerque Lima, learned of all of this and asked to open a parliamentary investigation into the actions of the SPI. The investigation report indeed revealed the atrocities committed against the Indians. "Torture comparable to that in Nazi camps," according to Attorney General Figueiredo Correia. Most of these acts were certainly not committed by agents of the SPI, but they were accused of letting them be perpetrated without denouncing them and without punishing the guilty parties. After having been convinced of the corruption and atrocities, the SPI was replaced in 1967 by the Fundação Nacional do Indio, the FUNAI.

As for our tribe, the health situation was disastrous after barely one year post-contact. Apoena Meireles attempted to organize a helicopter mission to one of our villages that had been devastated by a measles epidemic. However, the operation consisted merely of bringing anti-tetanus serum injections and Eucalpytine, a codeine syrup used to treat benign acute upper respiratory infections—medicine that was completely inappropriate

for the epidemics that we were facing.

Because no records were kept regarding the treatment results of their mission or regarding the identities of those who had been treated, our people were left unprotected against these foreign diseases, and yet the lethal impact of them had been known for centuries. In only three years, these epidemics reduced our population from five thousand to two hundred and forty.

Two hundred and forty!

Thomas Pizer, founder of Aquaverde, adorned in ritual painting with Almir's father, Marimop Suruí.
In 2006 Marimop and his wife Weytam adopted Pizer as their sixth son.
(Associação Metareilá Suruí)

THE SETTLERS

When I was born, which was only five years after the first contact, most of our families had been wiped out. The survivors described this period as a war that had been waged to eradicate them completely. It was a tremendous slaughter. Everyone grieved the loss of their brothers, sisters, father, mother, children, husbands, wives. I remember father Marimop's tears quite well as he brought up the people he had lost even much, much later. It was an unimaginable trauma. Compounding things further was the trauma of the profound change to our way of life which resulted from contact with Brazilian society and the FUNAI campaign to win us over and persuade us to accept their gifts that little by little we had come to depend on.

"However, not a single one of us felt sorry for ourselves," Marimop said.

Our one priority was to save ourselves from extinction and protecting, in law and in fact, the land that the whites had designated for us inside of the Aripuaná Park. This consisted of 3 million hectares (11,583 square miles) including Suruí land that had become the Seventh of September Reserve, as well as land belonging to the Cinta-Larga and the Zoró. The park was administered by the FUNAI, who by governmental decree had been designated to manage the use of mining resources. Since 1970, prospecting by individuals had been outlawed in Rondônia. This measure, we thought, would rid our land at long last of gold and diamond seekers who were invading it. It quickly became apparent that this was a means of giving the government free rein to sell permits to big mineral extraction companies.

In 1974, Apoena Meireles became the delegation head of the FUNAI of Rondônia at the same time that we were getting connected to the representatives of the military dictatorship, which had been established in Brazil in 1964. Meireles was unfortunately unable to do anything about the next hardship that we would soon confront. Settlers would arrive, encouraged by Emílio Garrastazu Médici (the President of the Federative Republic of Brazil from 1969 to 1974) and his government to move onto our land.

In order for you to understand these events, I must mention that the ideology of the 1970s was to open the Amazon rainforest to settlement and to solve Brazil's land rights issue by designating "the land without men for men without land," as President Médici described it. After the creation of INCRA (the National Institute for Colonization and Agrarian Reform) the government launched the construction of the Trans-Amazonian Highway. It was to cross Brazil from east to west and was going to reduce the isolation of these regions while encouraging development. Rumors quickly spread that every unemployed Brazilian who could get to this land inside the Amazon would have access to property and improved living conditions. In our region, reports issued in the framework of the government's settlement plan announced that the new BR-364 had covered regions whose volcanic soil was much more fertile than anywhere else in Amazonia, and that families of settlers who wanted to move there would have advantages such as property deeds, tools, seeds, loans and advice. This policy, whose slogan was "Security and Development," was unfortunately going to bring about another Indian genocide.

As early as 1971, a string of small settlements began to be built up along the BR-364 and more than 3,000 settlers moved into the town of Cacoal, near our territory. Most of them were small farmers from southern Brazil whose farms had been ruined by the spread of intensive farming of soybeans or coffee. Others were the inhabitants of urban slums who were drawn by the hope that this new El Dorado stirred inside of them. Real estate speculators followed them, and they rapidly hired hit men to eliminate their adversaries in the bitter fight to acquire new land. This is how in just 10 years, from 1970 to 1980, the population quadrupled and our Rondônia became a stage for the most violent battles over property in all of Brazil. We could even read in the press that the construction of the BR-364 had spurred a "land rush to virgin territory" that surpassed in speed and ferocity the settlement of the American West in the 19th century. The first figures on deforestation in the region were, incidentally, commensurate to that time in American history: from 120,000 hectares (296,500 acres) in 1975 to nearly 760,000 (1.8 million acres) in 1980!

Of all of the speculators, the Itaporanga company was at the heart of the biggest fraud that had ever been perpetrated against us.

Itaporanga was created in 1968 by four brothers from São Paulo named Melhorança. Their company illegally appropriated a section of our territory bordering the Ji-Paraná River. They did this despite the government banning entry into the Aripuaná Park that officially contained our territory. The Itaporanga company claimed that they had bought the rubber harvesting rights to the plot of land in question. Itaporanga then divided the land into parcels and sold the obviously falsified property deeds to one thousand settler families. Although the deeds were counterfeit, the settlers moved onto our land believing that they were the owners. You can probably imagine what happened next.

When we heard their chainsaws cutting down trees from the spot where our women were harvesting food, it became clear that we needed to demand not only that they be evicted but also that the thousands of hectares of land that had been taken illegally from us be given back.

After a thorough investigation, INCRA was able to file a lawsuit against Itaporanga. The Melhorança brothers' settlement project was deemed illegal, but the lawyer representing INCRA had to break it to the settlers that they were victims of a large-scale fraud and that they were going to be expelled. Many of these unfortunate people had borrowed money to buy the falsified land deeds. They had also worked very hard clearing and farming the land. As a result, most of them refused to leave, which then triggered more conflicts with our people. People were killed and houses were ransacked.

To try to assuage the situation, four people arrived on site promising us that they would find a solution: Humberto da Silva Guedes (the governor of Rondônia), Maurício Rangel Reis (the Minister of the Interior), Ismarth de Araújo Oliveira (the president of the FUNAI), and Hélio Palma de Arruda (the INCRA project Coordinator).

They kept their word, and in 1976 we finally obtained an official demarcation of land that allocated 247,870 hectares (612,500 acres) to us. This was the amount of land that had been stolen by the settlers and had never been restored to us. The governor also promised that the 300 families of settlers who were still on our land would be expelled. The governor was not able to keep his promise since, despite the intervention of the military police and the ultimatums issued by the FUNAI, the families resisted, and went so far as to destroy the signs that indicated our new official borders. Out of sheer exasperation, Anine, one of our leaders, led the attack on the FUNAI office in Riozinho. This was, admittedly, a solution borne of despair, the goal being to force the

government into protecting our rights. It only made the situation more toxic. Not even the skilled negotiator working for Apoena Meireles was able to defuse tensions that existed on either side.

By the end of 1978, the settlers closed the road from Riozinho leading to our land, preventing any FUNAI employees or any other vehicles from entering. They also took control of 10% of our land, where they built a saw mill and planted new crops of rice and coffee. We did everything we could to respond to these attacks by demanding that the state enforce the laws already in place, since we knew that the slightest violent incident on our part would trigger retaliation and would give the whites ammunition and fuel their belief that Indians were dangerous. But what had become of the law?

Ten years after first contact, several decrees had reduced our territory to less than half the area that was initially planned. One part of what was left had been illegally sold to settlers who refused to leave. To make matters worse, we also had to fight to hold back the encroaching prospectors drawn by the new discovery of diamond mines on the Cinta-Larga territory nearby.

In 1979, our chief, Itabira, went to Porto Velho on the Madeira River, one of the major tributaries of the Amazon River, to protest alongside our governor and Apoena Meireles, who was still the leader of the FUNAI in Rondônia.

"My people are hungry," he said. "The settlers use dynamite to kill our fish. They burn the forests where we hunt. What are you waiting for? Why won't you do something?"

The FUNAI had indeed promised that the Minister of Justice would remove the settlers.

"But they are still there!" Itabira insisted. "Will any effective measures be taken soon? Because if I tell my people to be patient and wait, soon enough they will no longer trust me and no longer obey me!"

Apoena Meireles answered that he would do his best to convince the government to find a solution.

In September we got a visit from Adhemar Ribeiro da Silva, the president of the FUNAI, who promised to remove the settlers. One month later, the director of INCRA made the same promise.

But months went by and the settlers stayed put.

Our people grew tired of waiting for legal intervention and we attempted a raid, forcing several of the settlers to leave naked and weaponless. Despite this, more than 80 families resisted leaving and we had to wait until 1981 for the FUNAI to finally obtain a court ruling with the ability to force the last settlers off of our land. It did not happen easily, of course, but they finally left and we were able to reclaim their villages, one of which was Lapetanha, where both my children and I were raised.

From then on, to get to our land from the town of Cacoal, we used the lines 7, 8, 9, 10, 11, 12, and 14, whose names came from the trails that had been used not only to make the very first contact but also to demarcate the boundaries between the indigenous land and the plots given to the settlers. After 1981, we were able to farm the coffee plantations that they had left behind which were located along each of these lines. In 1982, the income we earned from the first harvest made it possible for us to buy the products that had become so vital to us: clothing, tools and food.

THE POLONOROESTE PROGRAM

O n October 17, 1983, the demarcation from 1976 was ratified and approved by Brazil's president João Figueiredo. I was only four years old, but I still remember very clearly my father saying that at last our territory would be respected and protected. He did not suspect that another difficult trial was just around the corner.

This trial came under the name of Polonoroeste, a program created by the government at the beginning of the 1980s to accelerate the development of northwestern Brazil. Its first goal was to facilitate access to the States of Rondônia and Acre by paving the BR-364 from Cuiabá to Porto Velho, and then to Rio Branco. The eastern part of the road in Mato Grosso would also be doubled in length by the addition of a 400-kilometer loop in the Guaporé Forest in the heart of the Nambikwara land (the Nambikwara are a people in the south-east of Rondônia). Cândido Rondon first made contact with them when the telegraph lines were being installed. They had already been very afflicted by development politics since the flu epidemics in 1918-1919, and then in 1946 (after Rondon made contact) when measles slashed their population from 20,000 to merely 600. Was the Polonoroeste going to destroy their land as well? What would the impact be on the other indigenous populations?

The World Bank, which had been sought out in 1979 as one of the partners for this program and who provided no less than 1.5 million dollars of investment, seemed to be sensitive to these questions. The World Bank had agreed to finance up to 35% but, for the first time, the support was conditional and it urged the Brazilian government to protect the indigenous areas. The government also had to demarcate the land that had not yet been demarcated, and it had to allocate a part of the funds to the well-being and protection of the people who were victims of development.

Did the government honor these conditions?

The person given the delicate task of answering this question was Betty Mindlin, the anthropologist who, at the end of the 70s, had already condemned how close the

settlers had gotten to our territory and had always fought for the formal recognition of the Indians of Brazil. Unfortunately, the committee of experts that she assembled very quickly produced alarming reports. Even though the Polonoroeste program had indeed allowed for the delimiting of a few reserves for the Nambikwara and the Urueu Wau Wau people, 16 indigenous territories still needed demarcation, among them the one belonging to our neighbors the Zoró. Apoena Meireles established contact with the Zoró in 1977. The reports also revealed that there had not been a single attempt to stop the hydroelectric dam project on the Ji-Paraná River, nor to keep out the prospectors from our Aripuaná Park. There was also no attempt to keep the settlers away from the Igarapé Lourdes reservation where the Gavião and the Arara lived.

The Polonoroeste program was quickly characterized as a social and environmental disaster that had cost more than $1 million, of which only 2.5% had been invested in protecting the environment and only 1.4% had been invested in protecting indigenous people. The Polonoroeste program had also spurred a new wave of immigration in Rondônia that drew nearly 200,000 settlers per year. Our land was obviously not spared from the settlers' impact; it was occupied by small farmers and sought after by mining companies, and it became more and more difficult to keep control of it. Since our elders were unable to continue negotiating with the white people, they were forced little by little to cede their decision-making power to our younger generation. However, our young people's experiences resulted in a deep transformation within our society. They went into cities, learned Portuguese, experienced the dynamism of Brazilian society and discovered other farming methods and tools better adapted to a more intense work rhythm. However, at the same time they learned a lifestyle bereft of communal life.

I don't want to judge it. But the reality was that having this new lifestyle meant we needed to find some kind of income. This led to a complete change in our daily life, which had heretofore been balanced between having very few needs and a relative abundance of rainforest resources. To pay for the goods that we were dependent on from that point on, we had to commit to doing intensive work and adhering to very demanding schedules. However, the amount of time was still never enough to satisfy the needs of the new system of production.

"The rainforest has always taught us to adapt," my father would say. "We will live

through this transition!"

He was right. After having overcome the population catastrophe due to the first contact, we dedicated ourselves to studying Brazilian society, to understanding its laws and its free market economy. In just ten years, our people not only integrated all of these factors into how we live our lifestyle, but we also came to understand that it was very much in our interest to study and understand all of the societal codes of this new world.

Apoena Meirelles, 1969, sharing the chicha *drink made of manioc and fermented sweet potatoes.*
(Associação Metareilá Suruí)

THE SPIRITS OF
THE RAINFOREST

Today we are 1,400 and we may never again reach the 5,000 that we were before first contact, but know this: Marimop did not raise me to have hatred against the whites. Instead he taught me to respect our people and our traditions in order to make me a "true man," a *Paiter*.

As you know, among our people it is considered rude to beg for food because that would be to assume that the person does not want to share his food. Nor do we say thank you to a person who has given us something, just as we don't say thank you to someone for simply feeling loved. It's because of this wisdom that we are rebuilding our people. The education I received from my father was based on these principles. The first day that Marimop took me into our big rainforest remains one of my most beautiful memories to this day.

I had already ventured in the direction of the big trees at the edge of our village, but I had never been allowed to go any farther than that. Besides, my father had warned me that if I did, I might run into Lacapoy.

"If the spirit Lacapoy sees you, he will have a good laugh making you lose your way. And then he will lure you right to him!"

This had unfortunately already happened to my brother Agamemnon. Lacapoy had kidnapped him in the rainforest and held him there for a whole day and night. Marimop left to find him and let out a specific call that my brother, luckily, happened to hear. The poor boy hadn't been able to start a fire and was covered in nasty mosquito bites, but our *wáwá*, the shaman, treated them by applying a decoction of the bark of *niero chacup quépada*. "Only the *wáwá* can look at Lacapoy without going crazy," my father had told me. So, I should be very careful to not ever come across him.

On that day, however, I was in a hurry to go with my father into the rainforest. As soon as the rain stopped, I went outside.

"Can we go now?"

Once again, my father quelled my enthusiasm. "First we have to let the sky warm the forest up!"

As I waited, I ran my finger along the bark that was stretched across the base of the braided straw walls of our *maloca*, which was a technique we used to protect them from water. I squatted down in the doorway in front of one of the big black ceramic pots arranged around the communal fireplace. My mother, Weytam, was smiling as she watched me. She knew that I was going to make it all the way around our hut (which was 25m long and 8m wide, or 80 feet long and 13 feet wide, as tradition dictates) and that it would take quite a while for my finger to travel the length of the bark. She held a long bamboo spoon in her hand and stirred the yam soup (the main part of our meals). My father's second wife was crushing corn that she would use to make the flour that would go into other soups or for the *i*, our ceremonial drink.

The *Paiter Suruí* are polygamous, as you may know, but I must stress that they practiced avunculate marriage, in which a man must marry the daughter of his sister. Marriages between children of maternal uncles or paternal aunts (cross cousins) were also allowed, but not those between the children of maternal aunts and paternal uncles (parallel cousins) who were considered brothers and sisters.

The low thumps of the pestle slid into the background noise with the rain and my older sister sneezing (she had never tolerated the humidity very well). Sandra was making a necklace by stringing *tucumã* nuts onto a braided *tucumã* fiber. She had wound one end of the string around her big toe. Once she had tightened it she would polish down the nuts to a brown-black with a stone against the string until they were only one millimeter in diameter. The strand of nuts would be so supple and soft that the necklace would look and feel like leather. In between the *tucumã* pearls she sometimes strung monkey teeth or hedgehog quills. I preferred the necklace with the white pearls of tatou shell (an animal like an armadillo), which were the rarest ones.

"Pass me that basket at your feet," she said.

I looked at the *adô* basket that I had seen her braiding for more than an hour. We used those baskets to carry food from the garden and they circulated from one house

to another according to the changing harvests.

"I can't give you that basket," I told her, "I haven't finished tracing my finger the whole way around the *maloca*!"

Sandra shrugged and continued stringing the nuts onto her necklace. I paused to look at the ears of corn hanging next to the ripening bananas. Their sweet, sugary smell made me hungry but I kept my finger pressed to the bark and finally reached the back of our long hut. It was divided into small rectangular areas you would call rooms. Each space was sectioned off with simple posts connected to each other about a meter and a half off the ground by spokes of wood. From these we hung our hammocks next to one another and when evening came my mother would tend a small fire beneath them to keep us warm. Conversations would clip along while people chewed on corn cobs. Newborns were passed from one hammock to the next; boys, who are always hungry, would peck at the food stored in baskets at the entrance to the *maloca*; girls would learn to make hammocks and *agoiab* (straps to carry our children) or traditional belts, dyed with red pigment. These cozy scenes remain etched in my memory. I must say I feel a bit of nostalgia for it all. But let us get back to that particular day from my childhood.

I had just ducked under the battle arrows made by my father when he started doing a kind of dance.

"Watch my dance closely," he told me. "The *surucucu* is the most dangerous snake in our rainforest and I am acting out a fight with him. It is a fight to the death, and I am pretending that I am winning. This way I am warning him that he better not show up…"

I watched Marimop do the whole dance. His delicate muscles rolled beneath his skin with the flexibility of a jaguar. He kept his face fully concentrated on the battle with his invisible enemy. The fine line tattooed in a half-moon from one ear to the other (the mark of our tribe) betrayed none of his emotions. The red macaw feather threaded through the base of his nose did not quiver. It was beautiful. He had barely completed the ritual but I couldn't help asking him if this meant he could truly walk barefoot in the rainforest without fear of getting bitten by a snake.

"Learn how to do this dance," he replied, jutting his chin towards his left calf, "and listen closely to what I am going to tell you. Three years before you were born, I was forty years old, and I was bitten by a *cascavel*. As you know, they are extremely dangerous snakes and I was unconscious for an entire day. Even though the *wáwá* were able to

treat the bite with the plants of the rainforest, I was unable to walk for six months. I had plenty of time to reflect on why this had happened to me! The answer came to me in a dream. I was already in the kingdom of the dead, in *Gorakoy*. According to our origin story, souls cross a path riddled with obstacles. On their way, the souls might be attacked by a giant vulture, crushed by rocks, smothered in the excrement of a giant lizard or scared away by the presence of certain creatures with enormous genitals. The bravest souls can confront these dangers and arrive peacefully at their eternal home. But in order to one day complete these voyages in the best conditions, the living must never pronounce the name of the deceased, or else the dead will come back to haunt them. As for cowardly souls, or those who have committed incest, they die a second time and go to the village of useless souls.

"Among the living, only the *wáwá* can travel to the kingdom of the dead. To do this they use a winged stick *naraihb*, with its tip decorated with red macaw feathers and white sparrowhawk feathers. That is where Pálob, the god of our people, lives with different classes of spirits. Some have the power to make men sick and others, if they are called upon by the shaman, can heal them or keep illnesses away. Pálob is the one who orders the *wáwá* to begin healing rituals with the *ichoa* stones given by the water spirits. He also orders the wáwá to lead ceremonies to attract luck and abundance and to keep illnesses away, as in the *Hoeyateim* ritual.

"*Hoeyateim* takes place in the rainforest, and this ritual is led by the *wáwá*. The *wáwá* organizes the men into two circles. Those in the first circle hold four-meter-high bamboo poles, while those in the second circle play a very long flute. The spirits appear over the course of this ritual. Those from the river, the *goanei*, are summoned every other day, and the *gorei*, the spirits of the sky, are summoned on opposite days. They appear in the form of multiple entities, each one with its own songs and stories. We hear them in the voices of the shamans and everyone knows them. Thus, night and day, this music from the other world engulfs the village and the forest. From a distance, the long bamboo poles rise and fall to the rhythm of the sound of the flutes and the bells tied around the men's ankles. During the five days of this ritual, four shamans blow on the members of the tribe, as a benediction, and give them the sacred *ichoa* stones to protect them from illness. Next, everyone joins the circle and whistles in a very specific way. The breath is always connected to the soul, so it is very important to end this part of the ritual like

this. Long speeches that reunite the two halves—forest and the farming—come next. The final moment is when the flutes and the bamboo are broken and thrown deep into the forest so that people can no longer play them. This way they return to where they came from. And we will do the same thing, my son . . ."

My father caught his breath and then asked me if I was ready to hear the next part. Truth be told, I just wanted to go into the forest. But I listened respectfully.

"The *Paiter Suruí* can also go to the kingdom of the dead in their dreams," he continued. "That is what happened to me after the snake bite. I saw Xivagoti, the spirit that protects the *Gameb* clan, and then Ngouadob, the spirit protecting the *Kaban* clan. They each have their own music and come inside of you and sing it through you. This is how we know that they have arrived. And this is how our shamans receive their songs directly from the spirits of the waters, the skies or the underworld. So in my dream, Xivagoti was fighting with Ngouadob. Xivagoti told him, 'We are allies and we should be taking care of our people. Why did you not protect Marimop?' Ngouadob replied that I should have dropped my weapon. Xivagoti then helped me come back from the land of the dead. And then I understood that I had gone off hunting with the same gun that we used to kill our enemies. That was not right. I should have taken another weapon. That is why the snake bit me!"

Marimop had always said that that test had been an initiation. The year he spent secluded in a special hut after the snake bit him had changed him. They said that from then on he was a half-spirit and had become a spiritual leader even though he did not know how to read or how to write, just like everyone else prior to contact. As far as counting was concerned, the fingers on one hand were enough for him. Beyond five, we would simply say it was "a lot."

On the path that day, I discovered sounds and songs and scents that I had never encountered before.

"The forest is opening up to you," my father said. "Thank her for revealing this small part of herself to you."

I bowed my head respectfully.

"Do you see those long thorns on the trunk of this palm tree? Don't ever touch them. But you can eat the small black fruit, the *nitchin*. Their juice is sweet and quenches our

thirst."

He turned around.

"This palm tree here is called the *orcobèè*. Eating its fruit makes your hair grow."

I smiled as I glanced at his smooth, hairless arms. Quite naturally he began speaking to a big *abora* tree with its red, cone-shaped fruit. Soon I realized that he was introducing me to the *abora*.

"The spirit of this tree is called Saati. The *wáwá* say that he walks on a single foot because small animals ate his other leg. But don't be fooled, he is still very powerful and has the power to heal. He is also the symbol of the *Makor* clan."

"Did the tree tell you anything?"

"Well, for those who know the rainforest, the trees talk."

"And animals too?"

"Of course."

"And will the trees talk to me?"

"They only talk to those who know that they are talking."

"But now I know so why can't I hear them?"

"You will have to earn their trust."

"And how do I do that?"

"The father of the forest, the sprit Paidamata, will tell you."

I listened there for a long time. I didn't hear anything but the sound of insects, birds, frogs and leaves. It was all very deafening. And then the sound of my father's voice interrupting it.

"Look at this *mokaï* shrub with its round, light green leaves. If you rub these leaves on your arm, its spirit will protect you and make you stronger for carrying wood. If you pass the leaves in front of your eyes, they will also help you to find wood."

Marimop headed to another *mokaï* as though he was reuniting with an old friend. The eagle feathers of his *cocar* jostled to the agile rhythm of his steps. The feathers were arranged horizontally on braided straw and formed a black disk with white edges around his head. "This headdress gives us the strength of the eagle and the strength to confront animals that might attack us," he explained. "We wear the headdress as a sign of respect towards people we meet and it holds in it the memory of what we have done for an entire year."

Marimop tensed up suddenly.

"The forest has gone quiet," he whispered. "That is the sign that a predator is near, maybe a jaguar. A jaguar is the symbol of power for our people. The jaguar created humans and each of our clans from his own bones."

"How did he do it?"

"He breathed smoke into a tobacco leaf rolled around his bones and then the bones came to life."

Marimop ignored my wide-eyed bewilderment and he loaded his bow and motioned to me to stay behind him.

"This silence is proof that the animals and the trees can talk. With that silence, they can warn us that danger is coming."

I frowned.

"Silence can talk?"

"You must learn to listen to it . . ."

The conversation between the birds, frogs and leaves started up again.

"In each of these calls you can hear a message, and if you are in grave danger, for example, the toucan will tell you."

Marimop held his bow made of the *pupunha* palm and removed Jabiter, his battle arrow, from the quiver. Each warrior makes his own arrows from a rare bamboo called *yape*. The arrows differ depending on whether or not they are used for hunting, fishing, or fighting. But each one is marked by a carving and a decoration that identifies the maker of the arrow. My father's were decorated with cotton braids in geometric black and white designs. He showed me the tip of the one he was holding. It was spiked with the crests of waves peaking.

"Don't ever cut yourself on these tips. The *yape* bamboo that I carved them from was boiled in order to draw out the venom. If you cut yourself you won't stop bleeding!" He held the bow, which was much taller than him, in his left hand. It required much strength and skill to use it.

"You are a part of a clan of warriors, like me," he told me solemnly. "Ours is the smallest clan because many of our brothers were killed during the war with the whites. Now it is time for me to show you something . . ."

He pulled on the string of his bow made of *tucuma* fibers and *corahignap* bark.

"Listen carefully to the whistle when I release the arrow . . ."

He slowly loaded the arrow onto the bow and aimed for the trunk of a wild cacao tree that was at least ten paces away.

"Do you see that cacao pod on the upper part of the trunk?"

I had barely nodded when the string of the bow vibrated, high-pitched and clear.

"That sound tells us that the arrow will hit its target. You must practice and train until you hear that same sound . . ."

The fruit exploded when Jabiter made contact. I let out a cry of admiration despite myself.

"Will I get my own bow soon, Bà?"

Marimop smiled and nodded. Then he used his machete to make his way through a tangle of branches, seemingly without any effort.

"Do you see this liana, the *gapixág napoah*? It will be useful if you ever get hurt in the forest. The sap of its bark stops bleeding. And here is the water liana. You can drink its juice. But only cut it if you are thirsty. The forest is a living thing, and she will only respect you if you respect her. Without respect, the spirits of the forest will turn against you, like Lacapoy. We know him by his necklace of snakes and insects.

He showed me his necklace with several strands of *tucumá* bark beads that my mother had carved and polished.

"The power of a necklace comes from the intention of the one who gives it to you. This one protects me and keeps away bad luck because your mother performed a ritual that gave it this power. But someone with bad intentions could curse it before giving it to you. So never accept a necklace from a person whose intentions you do not know."

Marimop stopped in front of a tree that had at least ten long roots extending up from the trunk and into the earth about three feet away.

"This is the *panraah*, 'the tree that walks.'"

My eyes went wide again. "Trees don't walk!"

"Are you sure?"

"I've never seen them walk!"

"Does that mean that it cannot be done? Look at its roots. They pull the trunk of the tree around the forest to find sunlight and nutrients that the tree needs. It can move up to one or two meters per year."

I looked at the extraordinary tree for a long time and suddenly two things dawned on me. First, I should learn to look in a better way. Second, if a tree can walk, then nothing was impossible. Marimop's finger shot into the air.

"Do you hear that song?"

I strained to hear.

"Which one? There are so many!"

"The little rodent with brown fur, the *cutia*. He is saying that war will arrive soon. . . ."

Marimop listened again and added very gravely, "Your life will be a battle, my son."

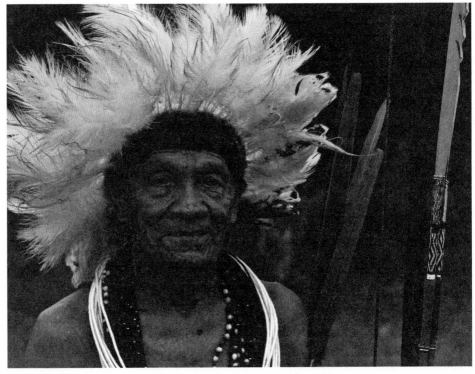

Marimop Surui, Almir's father and war chief.
© *T. Pizer, Aquaverde, 2010)*

CHIEF OF THE *GAMEB* CLAN

The *cutia* was right.

I began this fight when I was fourteen. I went to the meetings of the chiefs of the peoples of the Amazon, which included the Zoró—we knew how to get along when all of our interests were at stake—the Cinta-Larga, and the Gavião. The meetings took place in the Catholic Church in the town of Cacoal, but all sorts of religious groups were behind us at that point: Baptists, Catholics, Lutherans and representatives of the Assembly of God, whose missionaries came regularly in and out of our villages. I do not want to go on and on about this subject, but I must say that their influence profoundly altered our beliefs by inclining our shamans to abandon their ancestral rituals. Incidentally, the majority of them stopped practicing because the spirits that they were working with, as they told us, were jealous of the God of the new religions and they no longer wanted to speak to our shamans.

The missionaries also believed they were doing the right thing by forbidding the practice of our most important traditions, one of which is our coming of age ritual. During this tradition, our young people leave to hunt a jaguar and a golden eagle, alone. It was of course a bit dangerous, but the true purpose was not to succeed; what was important was to have experienced it. This is a beautiful lesson, is it not? The missionaries, far from approving of it, forbade tattoos, and then ritual body paintings, arguing that the *wáwá* were obeying evil spirits. If we did not go to church every Sunday, they maintained, if we did not read the Bible, if we did not listen to the teachings of their God, our souls would burn in hell. Was this fair? I cannot answer this question with any legitimacy, but I do know that this new dogma was imposed upon us little by little, and now, for example, the Christmas holiday is a part of our celebrations.

Some of us, myself included, are nevertheless still persuaded that our ancestral beliefs must be carried on.

"They give us our spiritual bearings, they are our roots," Marimop would say.

And I thank him for having continued to teach them to me. As I hope that you will transmit them to your children. I do not know if you want to decide the sex of your children, like our shamans have claimed to be able to do since very ancient times, but I am still going to reveal part of the secret to you. . . .

For example, to have a girl, they advise the couple to share a meal of cereal, high-fat foods and a slice of meat right before conception. To have a boy, the future parents must sit on *sobagey xaborgab* leaves and wear a necklace made of its seeds. I have never used this technique and I don't know whether or not my parents used these ways to decide on the gender of their children. They never wanted to talk to me about it! The fact remains that they had Iretana, Mopiri, Agamemnon, Sandra, Renato, myself and Noémi, one after the other.

At that time, a birth impacted and altered the lifestyle of the whole family. Thus, when I was born my father and my brothers isolated themselves for seven days in a *maloca* of braided straw built away from the village in order to center themselves and reflect. They also followed a diet free of bananas or corn since they were not expending any physical energy. But this rule of isolation also applied to young women during menstruation and to mothers who had just given birth (the blood of a new born was thought to be dangerous). To keep blood and death at a distance, a woman whose child had died also had to isolate herself for a period of six months. As for the young girls who had just reached puberty, a rite of passage was organized in which they had to remain in isolation. Each year after that, our "festival of young women" celebrated those who had gone through this trial.

With the influence of new religions, most of these traditions were lost, but still today the parents must obey a strict sexual abstinence while breastfeeding. Because breastfeeding is at the very source of how a family tree grows, the father and the mother are subject to a specific diet.

For the first ten days after the birth, the father eats only rice, cereal and milk—no corn. He must also forgo chicken for four months, armadillo for six months, and the *gongo*, the larva of the coconut borer, found in the fruit of the *babaçu* palm, until the child

can stand. Fish without scales, as well as tapir, wild boar, monkey and the fruit of the *pupnha* palm tree are forbidden until the child can walk. If the father does eat chicken, his baby will suffer eczema in the form of white skin patches; if he eats the fruit of the *pupnha*, the baby will have pimples; if he eats wild boar, he will have stomachaches; if he kills and eats a tapir, his child will go insane.

I observed that these rules seemed strange to foreigners with whom we had shared them, but these rules taught me one essential thing which you must remember above all else: what you eat affects not just you, but also your children. You must understand this responsibility, this interdependence of our bodies and of our souls. This is what our traditions teach us.

They also discourage us from marrying within the same clan. For example, we, the *Gameb,* had kept a very old tradition of intermarrying with the *Kaban,* but our women could also marry a man from the *Makor* or *Gamir* clans. However, they mustn't marry outside of our tribe. After contact with the whites, this tradition was unfortunately not always upheld and certain women married Brazilian men. As is expected, they followed their husbands and consequently their children lost their connection to our traditions. If this continues, we risk losing them all and we are in danger of seeing our tribe disappear little by little. As for the men, they are allowed to marry several women, even foreign women, but they must choose at least one from within our tribe. These rules are a way of maintaining our cultural identity, our existence as a people. But let us go back to my first meetings with the chiefs.

It was 1988 and the election of Tancredo de Almeida Neves three years prior had put an end to the military dictatorship, and I had just started my secondary education at the Cacoal high school. Chief Itabira represented the *Paiter Suruí* at that time and he was the one who had asked me to go with him. I already knew how our people had suffered tremendously from epidemics, wars, and the changes imposed upon our way of life by the presence of white people, but also by the reduction of our territory. At that first meeting, I knew our priorities were to ensure the safety of our people, protect our land, improve our health conditions, and develop educational programs. I had seen my father face these challenges again and again. And if he were still here, he would be sure to tell us about the day in 1989 when the *madeireiros,* the timber poachers, came to illegally

cut down wood on the outskirts of our village, Lapetanha.

While Marimop was walking along the route that led back to our village, he saw two of the timber poachers' trucks arrive. They were loaded to the brim with tree trunks that still smelled of sap. He was furious. He positioned himself in the middle of the road and motioned for the drivers to stop. They continued driving towards him, so he pulled out an arrow and nocked it. What a threat, standing there with the loaded bow! The first driver stopped his truck and ducked behind the dashboard. I should mention that absolutely no one could withstand my father's glare when he went into warrior mode . . .

"I am keeping these trucks. You will go back on foot!" he commanded.

The men did not need to hear him say it twice. They jumped out of the cab of the truck and ran as fast as their legs could carry them.

I still laugh thinking about this. Especially since the story doesn't stop there. When the timber poachers who were in charge heard about losing their two trucks, they went immediately to see our chiefs Anine and Itabira and demanded that Marimop give them back. Needless to say, he refused. Then they went to complain to the authorities. The next day at dawn, two police cars and four other vehicles arrived and surrounded our village. My father was furious. Would he choose his gun or his bow? He chose his bow, thinking that it would give him an edge. Even if it meant losing his own life, he would die a warrior.

He went out.

After finding the highest-ranking police officer, he nocked an arrow.

"No, no!" the man shouted, "we are here to talk!"

My sister translated since Marimop did not understand Portuguese. "Leave here right now. I will discuss nothing!" he told them.

The lieutenant backed away, but he tripped over a large rock. He fell down. Marimop was ready to shoot his arrow. He went and stood over him.

"I know that I am going to die, but if you don't put down your gun you will die first." The police officer apologized, stammering, "No, no, it's ok, we will leave!"

The next day, Itabira went to negotiate with the timber poachers. It's worth mentioning that he was selling them a lot of wood at that time and he did not want to lose that source of revenue. How could he have done that? To explain how, I need to tell you about a series of events in the mid-'80s. When I was ten years old, a giant truck arrived

in the village and it was the first time that I had ever seen one. It seemed enormous to me. Poachers stepped out of the truck. They wanted to see our chief. They had found a grove of hundred-year old mahogany trees in the west of our territory and had come to ask for permission to cut them down, in exchange for compensation, of course. We told ourselves that we all needed money, after all. And it was just one grove, just this once ...

Unfortunately, that first time led to further negotiations, and then more, and this easy money opened the door to a short-sighted vision of how we would manage our forest's resources. Very quickly the *madeireiros'* trucks rolled onto our land and in a few years, our chiefs had lost control of the situation. I do not mean to excuse their behavior entirely, but I must remind you that at the end of the 1980s, the resource management during the Polonoroeste program had deprived our tribe and others of the money allocated for health care and the commercialization of our products. Driven by destitution as well as not having a single public policy that guaranteed the integrity of our territories, some of us, such as Itabira, were strongly encouraged by FUNAI employees (who enabled logging in exchange for bribes), and had ended up giving in to the temptation to make deals with the timber poachers.

That is why, after a few days of discussion with Itabira, Marimop had to agree to return the trucks to the timber poachers ... but he kept the wood!

As you can see, I grew up amidst these struggles and witnessed many meetings with indigenous leaders. There was still a part of my training that I felt was indispensable, something that none of the members of our people had yet been able to accomplish: to study at a university. I can't thank the great indigenous leader Ailton Krenak enough. Given my very good grades and my virulent critique of the logging policies on indigenous land, he gave me the chance to join the Centro de Pesquisa Indigena, a research center designed to allow young Indians to attend the University of Goaiania near Brasilia. I studied Applied Biology there for four years. Believe me when I tell you that I took this privilege very seriously! With my degree in hand, I returned to my people who honored me by electing me chief of the *Gameb* clan. That was in June 1992, and I had just barely turned seventeen. I didn't know how weighty that responsibility would be, but I have always upheld it.

One of my first goals was to encourage our people to reconnect with our traditions, which had been eroded by the missionaries.

"Not a single tree ever grows without roots," Marimop would say.

So, we relearned how to do our ritual body painting. As you know, my favorite one is the jaguar, depicted by an oval painted around one's mouth and spots painted on the torso. The symbol of the jaguar is reserved for warriors and it gives the person wearing it the jaguar's powers: strength, flexibility and speed. There are obviously many other patterns, such as those given to people of high status, but it's important to know that they each have a different meaning and function. We get the dark blue pigment that we use to paint them by grating the bark of the *jenipapo* fruit in water. Once it has been boiled and cooled, it is applied to the arms, torso and legs with a piece of serrated bamboo. The painted dots and lines disappear after about three weeks when the skin naturally regenerates. Then you must start over, but these moments—when each person takes care of ritualizing the body of another—are an excellent way to address tensions within the clan. It is forbidden, however, to use the same pigment that has been used on an adult on a child who is younger than ten years old. This ensures that the adult, who has inevitably committed impure acts at this point, does not transmit them to the child.

My second goal was to develop an educational program that would allow our children to take classes in Portuguese, of course, but also in our own language, Tupi-Monde. For this, we supported a project coordinated by the Institute of Anthropology and the Environment via the Institute of Anthropology and Meio Ambiente (IAMA), which was designed to train Indian teachers to teach reading and oral communication in both languages.

My third goal was related to health. The victims of intestinal parasitosis, the flu, pneumonia, dehydration and diarrhea were primarily children. Adults suffered from tuberculosis, rheumatism, influenza or pneumonia and, because of the introduction of salt and sugar into our diet, high blood pressure, cardiovascular disease, and diabetes. Until 1989, it had been the FUNAI via the Cacoal administration that was responsible for providing health care for our people. From 1989 to 1991, the *Paiter Suruí* aid project that was developed by the CERNIC, the health center in Cacoal, took over by improving the level of assistance. And then from 1992, the PACA (the environmental protection organization of Cacoal) developed a training program for indigenous health workers

which resulted in a reduction of the mortality rate. For the first time since contact, we saw a significant population increase. As you probably have guessed, this news prompted a wave of relief among us. It was as though all of a sudden our people were no longer doomed to disappear completely, but rather that we could once more envision a future for ourselves. I do not know if what happened next was a direct consequence of this optimism, but over the course of that year, the year I turned seventeen, I married Adlanes, a white mestissa brazilian woman.

ASSERTING OUR RIGHTS

In 1994 when I was 20 years old, I became the coordinator of the indigenous movement of the State of Rondônia. I was the environmental leader for the Coordination of the Indigenous Organizations of the Brazilian Amazon (COIAB), an organization created to stand up to the FUNAI, where the corruption was getting worse.

It was while working at the COIAB that I was able to notice inconsistencies in the application of the laws and was able to denounce how the government of Rondônia was using the World Bank loans in ways that went against the interests of indigenous peoples. The goal of those loans was in fact to finance farming, health, and environmental protection projects as well as development projects for the region. Yet the government was not distributing any of the amounts designated for the Indians, nor had they done anything to preserve our land from the invading miners. Although the miners had quickly been discouraged by the paucity of gold that they found on our land, this was not the case for our neighbors the Cinta-Larga, who were still suffering from the violence caused by the discovery of diamond deposits on theirs.

We started asserting our rights by organizing several protests; however, these were unsuccessful. Other social movements like that of the seringueiros, latex harvesters and landless farmworkers joined us. But once more, we received no response from the government. Out of sheer desperation, we blocked the BR-364 at Porto Velho. One week later, the director of the World Bank asked us to come to New York to explain and elaborate on our demands. Before I left, I was given the honor of being designated as the leader of the indigenous movement. For the first time in my life I found myself in the United States sitting alongside the leaders of other movements. It was 1999 and I had just turned 25.

After listening attentively to us, the director of the World Bank decided to open an

investigation. The inconsistencies that we reported were quickly confirmed and the State of Rondônia had to return the amounts in question or else have the loans suspended. This solution seemed satisfying since we had finally received the money that had been reserved for us. It allowed us to bring electricity to our villages, which in turn earned us the support of the World Bank for other projects such as establishing health centers.

As you can imagine, we of course celebrated this victory, but a bitter taste was left in my mouth afterwards. How many more times would we have to fight to receive the money that was very obviously owed to us? How many times would we have to endure rules that were not our own?

I went to see my wife, Adlanes, to try to calm down. I asked her if she would go with me to the swimming spot we loved so much. It was where the river bed widened into a small lake surrounded by hundred-year old trees. Their branches dipped into the water that reflected thousands of shades of green. We carefully stepped into the water so as not to muddle the colors. The water was lukewarm and pleasant. As I stood there surrounded by all of that natural beauty, I told her what a shame it would be if our children one day no longer had access to this magnificent display of nature. The Amazon was so beautiful. When it became deep enough to swim, Adlanes came over and hooked her arms around my neck. I swam a few meters with her like that as though she could not swim at all. She started laughing as we pretended that she depended completely on me to stay afloat. And then we laughed together again when red macaws seemed to squawk in reply to our laughter.

I think that was where the idea began. Shouldn't our tribe free itself from its dependence on aid from the government?

We swam to the slopes of the riverbank covered in leaves. "Yes," I said to Adlanes, "our people should ensure that we can generate our own revenue, and without sacrificing our trees to the greed of the *madeireiros*."

From that moment on we decided we should dedicate ourselves to redirecting our economy towards solutions that involved managing our resources sustainably, such as organic farming, ecotourism and craftsmanship. Unfortunately, we still did not have any experience in these things or in managing a large-scale program where we could sell what we harvest. Without any other income, some of our people would prefer to continue accepting bribes from the timber poachers rather than count on the revenue

that would become a possibility if we were to use these new strategies.

"That may be the case," Adlanes agreed. "They are indeed concentrating more on the tangible income they get from deforestation instead of foreseeing the intangible but costly result of it."

Our neighbors the Cinta-Larga had very often accepted money from gold and diamond prospectors who had come onto their land like the timber poachers were coming onto ours. But in the end they realized that their extraction methods slaughtered the fish in their rivers. From then on, the money they received from the prospectors did not amount to much compared to what they would have to spend in grocery stores.

"We must convince our people not to make the same mistake," I told Adlanes.

I can still hear myself saying those words to her, almost in the way that one repeats a prayer. I did not know then that I would devote more than ten years of my life to the struggle. But I knew the struggle was just.

From there, we walked back calmly to the path that led us home to our village.

There still remain 95% of the Paiter Surui people's 600,000 acre territory that is untouched tropical forest, a treasure of biodiversity. *Georgio D'Imperio, Aquaverde*

Deforestation is still rampant in the State of Pará.
Magali Girardin, Aquaverde

PART II

One day, long ago, one of our four ancestors inseminated a calabash.

"Listen to the calabash," our ancestor said. At dawn, it exploded and a baby girl came out. At the same moment, another of our ancestors inseminated a tree.

"Listen to the tree," he said. At dawn it exploded and a baby came out: another girl. For many years, both girls grew up in the rainforest. The daughter of the tree was serious and well-behaved. She lived with her parents, ate very little and saved her virginity for the man that would marry her. The daughter of the bottle gourd was rebellious and bad-tempered. She fought often with others, ate voraciously and took many lovers. These two women had the power to transform quarrelsome people into animals. Thus, all animals are Paiter Suruí who were transformed by these women.

When they were old enough to marry, both women married the son of the Jaguar Woman. Every day he would leave to go hunting so he could feed his Jaguar Mother and his two wives. The rebellious daughter had the first baby, a son. Then the well-behaved daughter gave birth to another boy. One day, the Jaguar Mother went to collect wood in the forest with the combative/rebellious daughter and her baby. While she bent down to pick up a branch, she passed gas. The rebellious daughter burst out laughing. "If you make fun of me," her mother-in-law responded, "I will eat you!" The daughter continued making fun of her. So the Jaguar Mother ate her and took the baby home to her house. Several years later, while Jaguar Mother was grinding corn, the boy escaped to go live with the well-behaved daughter. The Jaguar Mother went to retrieve him but her well-behaved daughter-in-law took a smoldering stick and chased her away.

WHEN THE SUN REDDENS

I must have been about seven years old when one morning, my father asked me to sit in front of the door of our maloca, facing the rising sun.

"Wait for me here!" he said.

I asked him why but he left without looking at me. So I waited. At first I was intrigued, then I was angry, and then resigned. Our *wáwá* came over to me.

"Almir, what are you doing?"

"I am waiting for my father."

"Don't you have anything better to do?"

"No. He told me to wait for him."

The man smiled and then glanced down at a stump before sitting on it.

"Does waiting mean you are doing nothing?" he asked me.

I didn't answer. He asked me if my eyes were closed.

"No!"

"And your nostrils?"

"Of course not!"

"And your ears?"

"So why aren't you using them?"

""

"Do you see that *arinháy* shrub that's about five feet wide over there?"

I turned my head towards where he had motioned with his chin.

"That little scrawny one?"

"I know it doesn't look like much, but the skin of its roots contains a powerful remedy against stomach aches."

"How do you know that?"

"Observation is the key to knowledge, little one. But you must be humble in order to acquire it. You must accept that everything around you, as scrawny as it is, can teach you much more than you will ever know. Learn to observe the world around you with all of your senses.

I looked at him, suddenly very serious.

"So is that how our ancestors learned so much from the forest?"

He nodded.

"If you observe this way you will know the birds are transmitting messages to us through their songs—both good omens and bad. The animals warn us of danger. They make our lives safer and healthier, in harmony with Nature. The sound of the water from the rivers alerts us of rising water levels, it forecasts times of scarcity or abundance, and tells us the story of the fish. The hues in the sky and the colors of the rainbow tell us what weather is coming. The moon and the stars show us the paths to follow and warn us about hardships that could strike our villages . . .

I don't know what he said beyond that, and I don't know when he left me sitting there, but his words have stayed etched in my memory. And when at sunset my father arrived and asked me what I did while I was waiting, I told him that I had learned a lot—so many things! He smiled.

So this is how, we, the *Paiter Suruí,* know that when the sun reddens—which many people think is very beautiful—that it is actually the trees that are burning, that actually the animals are dying.

PLANTING TREES

Because I was very aware of how catastrophic the destruction of our forest would be, at the end of the 1990s I proposed that we establish an ethno-environmental assessment. The goal was to emphasize the value of the rainforest's cultural and economic potential, and also to demonstrate that it was possible to build a sustainable future using a long-term vision. The madeireiros, the timber poachers, wanted to make the forest profitable by cutting down trees? We, then, would have to create a model that combined protecting the environment with making a profit. The model would have to include a plan in which protecting our trees is a source of income. This way our people would no longer be tempted to sell our trees, and also our tribe's survival would no longer completely depend on external aid. I had no idea what shape this model would take, but I knew that implementing it would require us to consider a new political structure.

Until contact in 1969, our people elected clan chiefs who then elected a leader for the entire Suruí tribe. After 1969, most of the chiefs had died of illness and the survivors were not capable of electing any others. Historically, they had been appointed by the FUNAI until February of 1987, when we laid the foundation for the Metareilá Association of the Suruí Indigenous People. This new organization that included all of our clans was committed to evicting the timber poachers from indigenous lands, rejecting those of us who sold lumber to them, and electing leaders who were genuinely concerned with protecting the environment. Remember, metareilá in our tradition is the word for the clearing in which we meet to celebrate the Mapimaï, our Creation ritual. Our choice in using this name for our association was indeed a symbolic one.

The Metareilá association, which officially opened its doors in December 1988, became the governing institution of our people until 1998, at which point the association lost its authority. A few of our brothers actually continued making deals with the poachers

because of the lack of support and resources to support the community, which generated dissent and drove each clan to create its own separate organization. In 1999, the Gamir clan of line 14 founded the Gamirey Association and other associations, such as Parents and Teachers, which were dedicated to the development of educational programs.

We, the Gameb, chose to keep Metareilá running to represent our clan. It was already known as an important organization involved in the indigenous struggle and I thought we should preserve the visibility provided by the organization. This ended up being a good decision; as of this writing, having been in operation for 25 years, the Metareilá has become a major player in the struggle to assert our rights. Under the auspices of Metareilá and with its encouragement, Paiter women formed their own association. Despite the difficulties Metareilá had encountered, it had always striven to find solutions to our problems, defend the conservation of natural resources and support the implementation of governmental health, education and land projects. Among these I must explain Planafloro (the Rondônia Natural Resources Management Plan).

Planafloro was developed at the end of the 1980s, and was intended to be the model for a new generation of "green" projects created to promote environmental protection and to rectify the mistakes of the first plan, Polonoroeste, which now was seen as an ecological catastrophe in the eyes of the international community. The World Bank, being one of Polonoreste's partners, was in a difficult position due to this criticism. As a result, the World Bank suggested financing a 250 million-dollar plan, but this time, under certain conditions. The new funding would also have to be dedicated to improving the local infrastructure. To obtain the funds, the State of Rondônia would first have to accept an initial land zoning plan that would later be revised by Planafloro. This zoning plan categorized six regions that increased in levels of protection, which would significantly decrease deforestation as well as provide total protection for the remaining forest zones.

Planafloro was approved in 1993 by the legislative body of Rondônia. Its implementation was a true innovation for the Amazon. There would nevertheless be some obstacles, as we will see, but I must now get back to the story of our tribe.

In order to represent all of our clans, we created the Suruí Forum of Indigenous Organizations in 2003. This unfortunately was not enough to resolve all dissent within our group, for some among us—only a small minority, it should be noted—who wanted to

make a profit off the forest continued to make deals with the madeireiros. Because of this, the national press started to designate the Suruí as "the Deforestation Indians!"

It was very sad to see these articles when the majority of the tribe understood why we needed to protect our rainforest. But emotions aside, as their chief, my task was to find a solution. When I asked myself what these men wanted, deep down, out of selling the wood from our land, it was clear that they want what every one of us wants: to feed our families. Therefore, my responsibility was to provide them with another way to do that. So, I sat down with them and asked them whether other solutions for generating income existed aside from deforestation. That is how, in the beginning of the 2000s, each of the clan leaders was invited to brainstorm ideas.

One suggested bottling water from our springs and another suggested harvesting gold or diamonds that our land might contain. My suggestion was to plant trees. I remember quite clearly the silence and then the laughter that followed my suggestion, even from members of our own clan. I naturally asked them why they were laughing. I must admit I was a bit angry.

"So you don't want to plant trees?" I shouted.

They all laughed again. And then, all together, they said, "Planting trees in the Amazon rainforest is like pouring water into the sea!"

This time I laughed with them, realizing how absurd my proposition was. Not the idea itself but how I presented it. In the end, they congratulated me. Yes, our clan would plant trees in all the areas that had been deforested and would eventually convince the other clans to join us.

The fourth clan leader unfortunately wanted to continue selling our timber. I told him that at this rate, pretty soon we wouldn't have any timber at all and that if we didn't develop other sources of revenue soon, we would become totally dependent on external aid. And what would we do if they ever cut it off? What would we live off of then? The lack of long-term vision was absurd—as absurd as not adhering to the precise times that we fish with the timbó—which we never do more than once a year!

But what a pleasure it is to walk together along the rivers on our territory when we do go fishing—Branco, Lobo, Gapo, or Ribeirão. So many memories rise inside me, you see, when I think of those names. I could sing songs about every bend in the river, each sand bar, every glint of moonlight, and in so doing create a map as precise (but much

more poetic) as a satellite photo! We craft bundles of tamboriu branches and markab lianas that we throw into shallow pools. Once the bundles are floating on the water's surface, we simply arm ourselves with sticks. Then we wade into the river up to our calves. Next, we laugh and shout while we beat the sticks with all our might to draw out the whitish liquid in the branches that puts the fish to sleep (but does not hurt them). And what a joy it is afterward to see the tribe reunited at the heart of the big maloca for the Ytxaga celebration that comes after this fishing!

However, it is imperative that this fishing be done only during the dry season in shallow pools where the water will evaporate and where the fish would eventually asphyxiate anyway. We only eat fish with scales, since the others are considered carriers of disease. Electric eels are the one exception . . .

"The jolt from an eel can kill a human," my father told me to discourage me from touching them. After hearing this, I was torn between the pleasure of fishing and the terror of death by electrocution, so I developed a technique all my own: I hunted the eel with my bow, and when my arrow hit the eel (which was rarely the case), I would ask my father to trap it in a big fishing net.

The fishing method most commonly used today includes a nylon fishing line and bait, but we have always upheld the value of sustainable management of the forest's resources, and we respect specific schedules for fishing, hunting, and for each challenge we tackle. Being aware of this will spare you a lot of failures. For example, knowing that the tatou is a nocturnal animal will save you time trying to hunt it in the daylight.

Without this knowledge, we would no longer have fish or game and the trees would disappear. Our culture would be wiped away and we would simply no longer exist. Wouldn't that be a tremendous loss? I have become all that I am because of all that my father taught me about the forest. So this is what I want to explain to as many people as I can. Have I told you, for example, to what extent night hunting became an important lesson for me? The Suruí only hunt at night on certain occasions and only during a full moon. I will explain . . .

When my father took me into the forest, we only had one torch to light the path. Since the tatou can detect the smell of fire, you have to light the torch at exactly the right moment and put it out as soon as you find one. Each hunter, therefore, had his own technique—a strategy all his own resulting from several years of experience. With

no other source of light than the moon, Marimop ran barefooted behind the tatou until it was exhausted. I was terrified to do this in the dark, yes, but I learned to trust my other senses, not just my vision. I developed my own strategies. My favorite involved hiding and then imitating the call of the animal I was hunting. The best moment was when I would hear it call back to me. This calling back and forth could go on for hours. This method and our traditions taught me that having a goal is like hunting an animal: you have to know its habits well to be able to have a good chance of seizing it. Each experience is therefore a challenge—never about power or money—but rather the joy of having learned something!

Among the Surui, as you know, challenges are at the very foundation of our clan's inner workings. They strengthen our ties to one another and are a way of communicating that allows us to assess how in harmony our relationships are.

For example, if a member of our clan builds a bow that is more beautiful than mine, I lose. If I bring home less game than him, I lose. If I take up a challenge without taking our traditions into account, I lose. But it is by showing me that he can do better than me that he shows that I have lost. Not by criticizing what I have done, nor by putting me down in the eyes of our people. Each person must comply with the decision of the whole and accept it. All of our actions are weighed out in this way. In the same way, if I lose a challenge again and again, I demonstrate my inability to lead the clan. Since I am the leader, I am continually being tested, like the day when we came back from hunting with the men of the Kaban clan.

Our women and the children old enough to come had accompanied us. (Even though the children are not allowed to use weapons, they help lead the game into the traps.) Our favorite prey are collared peccary, wild pigs, monkeys, ant-eaters, coati, armadillo, and different birds such as the curassows (hocco de Daubenton, a big gallinaceous ground-eating bird) the jacu, and the partridge, especially preferred by women who have just given birth. However, certain animals like jaguars, alligators, snakes, amphibians, eagles, rats, ducks, capybara rodents, toucans and some monkeys are forbidden foods (deer and tapir are forbidden especially for children).

So, on that particular day, we had decided to go hunting with our guns. We chose our guns because the yape bamboo that we carve our arrows from had been progressively disappearing. So on that day, we were able to hunt down four peccaries. After having

cut up the meat, the Kaban clan leader challenged me to distribute it "fairly." Within our tribe, this does not mean "in equal amounts" but instead refers to the way that the Kaban clan was expecting to receive it. And therein lies the subtlety of the challenge. If I didn't distribute it the way that they wished, not only would I lose the challenge, but also, I would lose face for my whole clan. So, I took great care in how I distributed it!

These challenges exist to ensure that we stay on guard and maintain respect for our traditions and fulfill our role in society by being the best we can be. If we do not, the other person lets us know and we must then find an honorable solution that will prevent our clan from losing face. That is how we have shaped our society since the dawn of time.

You must certainly remember, my children, what the FUNAI administrator said when he was asked by the clan leaders for a higher daily wage for replanting the forest. He explained that the organization was not rich, and that it would be difficult to honor our request. He actually justified himself and then continued complaining. For the Paiter Suruí, a leader would never adopt this defensive stance. He should have instead been firm and said, "No, that is not possible, for this or that reason." If I had taken his approach, I would have lost the challenge. To not be clear and firm shows weakness and demonstrates that you are not able to lead a clan.

You may not have known about this, but during one of my trips, a temporary chief had to be elected. We knew that my brother Renato wanted the role. We also knew that among us there were many other men who were much more competent than he was. But we wanted to give him a chance so we presented him with the challenge of leading our group. It quickly became very clear that he was not capable of taking on the role. However, everyone played along and no one objected to his decisions. He realized on his own that he was not capable of leading. Despite this, no one held it against him, but that challenge was a way for him to discover his true place within our group. The Paiter Suruí give everyone the opportunity to find their proper place.

Our clans also issue challenges among ourselves to determine how capable we are in confronting an opponent or solving a problem with finesse. The Mapimaï festival, our annual Creation ritual, is the prime occasion to redefine the regulations and relationships between the clans. We had abandoned the festival for twelve years but resurrected the celebration again in 2002 to pay homage to our brothers who had been killed. We also celebrate Ngamangaré in honor of our newly planted crops, the Weyxomaré in honor of

our body paintings, and the Hoeyateim which is led by the wáwá to control the spirits of the village. We practice the Lawaãwewa to celebrate the construction of a new home and the Ytxaga for fishing with the timbó. But let me come back to the Mapimaï festival, which takes months to prepare.

For this occasion, our tribe is split into two groups: the Kaban clan on one side, and the Makor, Gamir, and Gameb clans on the other. While the iwai group that works in the fields prepares huge quantities of chicha (our traditional fermented drink made of corn or yams) the group in the forest goes to the location where the ceremony will take place, the metareilá, to don themselves with body paintings, ornaments and ritual necklaces. The first day of the festival, those in the forest form a huge procession leading to the village while singing our ritual songs. The wives of the leaders of the ceremonies hold torches and are attentive to keeping the flames alive. (If they did not it would mean a death in the near future, or Palob, our god, refusing to continue to protect our homes.) Once the procession has arrived at the village, the iwai group that prepared the chicha offers some to the forest group in exchange for gifts. But if these presents are not what the iwai group is expecting, the forest group loses the challenge. Likewise, if the forest group is not able to drink all of the chicha, the planting group loses! To win the challenge, each group must know how to anticipate what the other group is expecting. With this, we learn how to be attentive to one another . . .

So, starting as children we learn to take into account that our actions affect not only ourselves but everyone. We experience the group as an interdependent entity that must think together before acting.

But be careful, my children, these rules are the rules of our tribe. When they come into contact with another culture, there are sure to be many surprises. . . . Around the time of first contact, for example, a white chief offered coffee to our chief. Ours interpreted this as a challenge, so he drank the coffee in one gulp. Convinced that our chief wanted more, the white chief served him more. Ours was convinced he should take on the challenge, so he drank it. The white chief wanted to be polite and filled his glass. Determined not to lose face for our clan, our chief drained the glass again. But the white leader filled the glass . . . you can imagine the next part.

Our chief had never been so agitated!

THE 50-YEAR PLAN

On my quest to find a way for our people to become economically independent, the idea of a sustainable management plan for our forest resources gradually developed. We needed a plan for the next fifty years that would ensure stable sources of income and a future for our tribe. It took time to lay the foundation for it, but I finally succeeded in convincing the Gameb, and then the rest of our clans to move forward with the plan.

Among other things the plan included the sustainable production of Brazil nuts, copaïba oil, organic bananas and organic coffee. The product sales would be managed by a cooperative rather than by individuals, as was our custom. This is due to the fact that, in the 1990s, the price of coffee went back up, which convinced us to start cultivating it again. The plantations were family-run, and part of the harvest was roasted in Cacoal in machines given to Metareilá by the FUNAI, and the rest of the harvest was sold directly by the families to companies who were quick to take advantage of their poor knowledge of market prices. The cooperative would therefore be a way of securing prices and providing a structure that could best negotiate the price of coffee sales with wholesalers.

The plan also included the implementation of environmental services such as eco-tourism. A part of the money earned would go to support the indigenous association's efforts to improve education, culture and health. The other part would be saved and would allow us to amass funds towards our goal of being financially autonomous. We would do all of this in partnership with other groups or political systems so that we would be independent while still remaining integrated into the whole. The mentality was not "I don't need you," but rather "We all need one another's knowledge, but are not dependent on it." This was our vision of what I call "responsible" integration.

In 2004, our 50-year management plan was ready. Nevertheless, we still needed to

find international partners. I only had one old computer, but I was able to get online. I typed "Amazon reforestation" in a Google search bar and the first result that came up was a Swiss organization called Aquaverde. According to the website its objective was reforestation alongside financial compensation. Could you imagine my joy? It was exactly the kind of financial strategy that I had wished to orient our tribe towards. I sent them an email on the spot.

A week and then ten days went by without a response. Thinking that the recipient of my email might not speak Portuguese, I had my message translated into French when a French man passed through our village. That time, I got a response from Thomas Pizer, the president of Aquaverde, the organization that became the first European organization to pledge their support to us. This was a huge step, you see, since this proved that it was indeed possible to generate income by planting trees instead of cutting them down. And little by little, this money would free us from the helplessness that comes from being dependent on government aid.

At the same time, I learned that the Amazon Conservation Team (ACT) had worked with the Xingú Indians, a people in Mato Grosso living on the headwaters of the Xingú River (which we will come back to later). Together, the Xingú Indians and ACT worked to create a cultural map of their ancestral land that showed their sacred places, historic sites, and hunting grounds, among other things. I immediately thought that a cultural map like this could promote our own culture and help me develop our resource management plan. So I got in contact with ACT in December of 2004. ACT's director, Vasco van Roosmalen, who has since become a friend, quickly agreed to support us with a grant from the Annenberg Foundation to develop a cultural map of our territory.

You have heard this before, but once more I will say it: this grant meant that it was possible for our tribe to get the means to generate our own revenue. What's more, the map project and the temporary jobs that it created helped me get the support of all of our clan chiefs—for the first time!—for a moratorium on logging on our land. To those who were reluctant, I told them this:

"The grant money will likely not compensate for the income we lost to illegal timber poaching, but this is honest money, the fruits of labor fulfilling to our tribe. It will also set an example for our youth."

It seemed that everything was getting better for us and for the other tribes as well.

However, we represented just a fraction of Brazil's population—0.42% according to the 2010 census—therefore we had very little political influence. We knew, of course, that the whites had an enduring prejudice against the Indians and we certainly had our own against them. But we were trying to improve our image in their eyes by demonstrating again and again that our expertise in the rainforest and its resources—an expertise that we alone possess—could benefit everyone. This seemed to work. Opinion polls started showing that the Indians' image was indeed improving. But despite all of this, very few Indians were able to win elections.

Out of the 350 Indian candidates running in local elections in 2000, only 75 were elected: one mayor, 3 members of national congress and 71 city councilors. At the national level, Antonia Ferreira da Silva who was elected senator in 2003 was the only Indian to have become a part of the legislative body since the election of Mário Juruna as Federal Representative (1983 to 1986). Clearly, we needed to improve this track record, especially here in Rondônia. However, the new governor, Ivo Cassol, would bring us new challenges.

Cassol was elected in 2004 and quickly decided to stop soliciting aid from the World Bank, which had always allocated a part of their funds to us. Had the control that the World Bank imposed on the management of government finances become too restrictive? I can't say for sure, but let's just say that Cassol preferred relying on the money from deforestation by giving political support and financial backing to the timber poachers. Clearly, this was a catastrophe, but it nonetheless drove me to reflect on our situation and to eventually understand that these people were acting mostly out of a lack of understanding about what constitutes equitable and fair development. After realizing this, it was clear that we wouldn't be engaging in a struggle with weapons, but rather in a struggle to change people's mindsets and raise awareness by strictly enforcing the laws.

THE FIRST DEATH THREATS

In order to ensure the survival of the tribe while waiting for projects to be implemented that would allow us to generate our own income, I continued to appeal to non-governmental organizations that might be able to help us. That is how, in 2005, we received financial help from Aquaverde. At this point, it is important for me to thank Thomas Pizer, the president of Aquaverde. Now I will tell you the story of how Thomas Pizer became my brother.

During his first visit to our village in December 2006, my mother Weytam went over to Thomas. She had two cotton fiber necklaces in her hands, one red and one white. After she spoke a few words to him, she placed the necklaces around his neck. He thanked her warmly but did not realize what an emotional moment this was for our people who were watching her make this gesture. The specific type of necklace she gave him was reserved for Suruí chiefs and was never offered to white people. Weytam maintained her composure and explained that she had had a vision the previous night that Thomas would provide substantial help in the battle that the tribe and I were in the process of fighting. Weytam would therefore adopt Thomas as her son in order to secure his place among the Suruí people. Then Marimop welcomed his adoptive son and named him No Honira Iuwai, "the man who comes from the great mountains," referring to the mountains in Pizer's native Switzerland. Perpeira, our *wáwá,* then gave him the ceremonial name Naraykapamib, "spirit of the tree that protects with its branches." From then on, Marimop and Weytam have always considered Thomas as one of their children. Thomas took up his role and worked for the good of the Suruí people, both with his knowledge and with his actions. From that point forward, Thomas Pizer was a part of the Gameb clan, assuming his role as our brother.

In addition to the support from Aquaverde, NORAD (the Norwegian Agency for

Development Cooperation) and USAID (the United States Agency for International Development) provided financial support so that we could address our medical needs and expand our projects. The Brazilian NGO Kanindé (Association of Ethno-Environmental Defense) led by my second wife Ivaneide, donated 1,950 tree seedlings that they received as payment from the madeireiros as a part of the fine imposed by the Porto Velho court. That was, of course, the first time that we had received any compensation from the timber poachers! It would also be the last. But no matter. Those tiny trees would be replanted at the start of the rainy season, as they should be, and the money from Aquaverde would allow us to pay those among us who would be doing the work.

We met to decide on the tree varieties that we should prioritize replanting. Our women advised us to start with the trees that the madeireiros' logging had impacted the most: cashew trees, cerjera, mahogany, pupunha, cacao trees, babaçu, tucumã and tamborio (whose bark we use to prepare the timbó for fishing). We also decided to plant them in the same areas where they had been cut down and where they would have the best chance of being able to grow back.

The first tree designated for our reforestation project was a mahogany tree.

We planted it on an expanse of capoera—a stretch of brushy undergrowth resulting from deforestation—right next to our village. As soon as the soil covered the seedling's roots and its little trunk could hold itself upright, we began to sing a song for the rebirth of the forest, stomping out the rhythm with bells around our ankles. Among our people, a chant or a song is always better than a long speech. For nearly any occasion we allow the high-pitched sounds from our throats to make the rainforest resonate with metallic trills punctuated with long final notes. During the Mapimaï, each participant invents a song in which he must communicate a message to the tribe. The message can be about a challenge, war, a strategy for the continuation of the clan, or a way to save the rainforest, but the messages are never an attempt to settle any small grievances. (All of the *fofoca,* literally "small vomits", are settled elsewhere). Next we all sing together, each contributing our different music, and the song of the Mapimaï become a way to resolve our disagreements and to redefine the relations between clans.

The following year, the Aquaverde organization increased its donation, which allowed us to plant even more trees. I also used the internet and YouTube to condemn the illegal conduct of the madeireiros. Since the moratorium forbidding logging on our land, our

people were no longer making any deals with them, so the poachers had decided to fell trees in secret. Of course, they demanded that I stop condemning them on the internet, but I continued. So, then they tried to bribe me. To no avail, as you already know. Next, they tried to bribe the other Indians—a method that they had often used to pit us against each other (which I must admit is unfortunately very effective). However, I know my people very well, and in this instance, at least, I was able to de-escalate the situation. But I was going to pay for it.

One evening, the telephone rang. A man's voice on the line said that if I continued to prevent my people from making deals with the madeireiros, they would put a price on my head. I clenched my fists and tried to hold back my rage, but I still ended up insulting the unknown voice on the phone. I don't remember what I said, but I remember very clearly the fear that replaced my rage as soon as I thought of my children, and when I thought about our people and the rainforest. And then the rage returned. So, the timber poachers wanted my head? Well, they had forgotten that taking up challenges are my people's favorite game! Taking on challenges has been the backbone holding my people upright after nearly all of us were slaughtered. Very calmly, I hung up the phone.

A few days later, I learned that a reward of 200,000 réals (approximately $100,000) was being offered to any person who could kill me. The news spread quickly and even my children found out about it. I was evacuated to Manaus in northern Brazil, and then to the United States, where I was able to secure more funding for our project. From there, an incredible adventure awaited me.

GOOGLE

It was 2007 and I had just arrived in California where I had been invited to give a talk to promote our cause. I had brought with me the cultural map of our territory, thinking that it would make the problem at hand more concrete in the eyes of these people. I didn't know at the time exactly how useful it would prove to be.

One day I went with my friend Vasco Van Roosemalen into Silicon Valley—he had left his position as director of ACT (Amazon Conservation Team) in order to run the organization ECAM, (Equipe de Conservação da Amazônia). We were passing right in front of Google headquarters. As I told you, I had been using Google's search engine to get in contact with potential partners. But just before being evacuated, I also connected to Google Earth. It was the first time I had used it, you see, and people said that I had done exactly what everyone else did. I spun the world map and zoomed straight to our territory. But instead of finding our villages, I found a kind of green oasis marked "uninhabited region." Our region was roughly the shape of a trapezoid in the middle of a yellow and gray sea representing deforested land and farms. I immediately thought that Google Earth could be a tremendous tool to help us monitor our forest. They had nevertheless omitted one essential thing: our very existence.

While we were standing outside of Google headquarters, I asked Vasco to schedule us a meeting. Shouldn't we inform them that an entire people is living in their "uninhabited region"? Couldn't they also help us in some way? Vasco tried to dissuade me.

"All they are going to do is help you right out the door!"

I insisted. Something told me that it would be good for us. Vasco ended up giving in, but he wanted to call them instead. Just before dialing the number, he turned to me and said, "You're completely crazy."

Of all the times I had heard this, this time I thought he might be right.

After a few rings that seemed to last an eternity, someone picked up and Vasco began our story. I didn't understand what he was saying since I don't speak English, but I watched a smile creep little by little onto his face.

"Did it work?"

"Don't start celebrating just yet," he said as he hung up. "All I got was an interview."

"Just like I thought! With whom?"

"With the director of Google Earth Outreach, the humanitarian branch of Google."

Once more, my face lit up. Vasco scowled.

"We got this meeting because I really insisted, but don't get your hopes up."

The next day after waiting for more than an hour (although we had arrived very early) the door to Rebecca Moore's office opened. I was wearing my cocar, a headdress of black eagle feathers with white tips that we use for important meetings. After having briefly examined my headdress, Rebecca Moore spoke. Vasco turned to me, looking worried.

"She only has thirty minutes to talk to us. That isn't enough time, is it? I'll have to translate everything. . ."

I thought for a few seconds. "I am ready."

He nodded. I took a deep breath and dove in.

"According to a report of the Food and Agriculture Organization of the United Nations, Brazil has lost 20% of its rainforest over the last ten years. This has been essentially due to intensive farming, large-scale soybean production, and wood consumption by a population that is ever-growing. If we allow this trend to accelerate, what will be left of the grand Amazon rainforest in fifty years? We, the Paiter Suruí people, began defending the rainforest first with our bows and arrows, and next with pencils and paper. Now we have computers and solutions to propose to you. Will you take the time to hear them?"

The end of the thirty minutes drew near but Rebecca Moore asked me to go on. I took out the map of our land that I had rolled inside a mailing tube.

Four hours later, not only was Rebecca Moore still listening, but she had called in the heads of other departments. Among them was John Hanke, to whom she introduced me. He is the creator of the software Keyhole which was bought in 2004 by Google and renamed . . . perhaps you guessed it: Google Earth. I was very happy to meet him, as you can imagine, and I congratulated him before asking him the question that would not leave me alone.

"Why does our land appear uninhabited when you zoom in using Google Earth and

Google Maps? When you point to the city of Cacoal that is right next to us, you see videos, photos and museums. Isn't it also important that when zooming in on our land that you see that an entire people has lived there for generations, with our traditions and culture, and that we are struggling to stay alive?"

The room fell silent for several long moments. Then, she spoke words that reassured me. "We must fix this error."

"Don't get your hopes up!" Vasco said to me again once we had left. "Their interest will not necessarily result in any kind of substantial help."

I didn't have time to answer him. His phone rang. A journalist from the *Washington Post* was on the line. He had read an article in the *Smithsonian* magazine that portrayed me as the new Chico Mendes, the great Brazilian trade union leader. I nearly choked because the many fights that Mendes led to save the Amazon rainforest—as well as the indigenous people living there—had cost him his life in 1988 when he was assassinated at age 44 in front of his family.

The murder had been commissioned by a big landowner and shook the entire world. It spurred the creation of 20 or so forest reserves that covered more than 20 million acres (30,000 square miles or 8 million hectares) in the northern Brazilian state of Acre where he lived.

The *Washington Post* journalist wanted to know what I thought about all of this. I naturally had a lot of admiration for Mendes, but this is how Vasco translated my answer: "Almir Suruí is not Chico Mendes. He doesn't want to become a dead hero. But he is currently in California looking to build some partnerships and he just left Google headquarters."

"Really?" The journalist was surprised. "Google is going to help his cause?"

"No, no, we don't know anything yet!"

The next day I took a plane to Geneva. I had been invited by Thomas Pizer, who is like a brother to me. It was my first trip to Europe and I was very happy for it. I had just arrived when Thomas told me that a *Washington Post* article had reported that Google was going to help the Suruí. He said that journalists from around the world had already called him asking to interview me. How did they get his number? I still don't know.

Another thing that I never found out was whether or not Google ever truly had the intention to support our project. However, all the articles garnered them much publicity

and I imagine that that kind of pressure convinced them. They called me a little while later to tell me that, as a part of her work with Google Earth Outreach, Rebecca Moore was prepared to send us a dozen computers. She was also sending people to train us to create an interactive historical and cultural map of the Suruí land. This way, Google Earth would help our tribe share our knowledge about the rainforest. Google would also finance GPS linked to the internet via satellite to map each parcel of our land, creating a better way to monitor and pinpoint illegal deforestation.

That day I lamented not having the privilege of being among my people to share my joy. And then I told myself, "Why must I be forced to run away? Who is really in the wrong? Me, or the madeireiros who are destroying our heritage? Why give in to their threats?" My people had been confronted by much worse and after all, no battle was ever won without some kind of loss!

A few days later, I was back in our village.

"You could have gotten more than that from Google!" certain people told me.

I answered that not only was this partnership going to allow our youth to have access to new technology, but that it would also give us international visibility so that we could finally make our cause known. What happened next proved me right.

I was invited to many countries to give talks about our 50-year sustainable management plan for the rainforest. Each time they would say, "That's the Indian who's partnering with Google!" In the international press the headlines referred to us as "high-tech Indians." That was a bit of an exaggeration, I will admit, but it allowed me to put out the call for help to get us the support we needed to repair what we'd lost to illegal deforestation.

The international organizations that had been supporting us responded. Thanks to their donations, along with those of the groups Kanindé and Aquaverde, we were able to buy tree seedlings and replant more than 100,000 of them. It will still require more time to reach our goal of one million that we decided on in our 50-year plan, but it is coming along. Today, with Google Earth Engine, it is already possible to see a tiny dot on the animated map inside the vastness of Brazil: our tribe. The program shows photos and 3D videos of the rainforest and our villages as well as our history and our traditions.

The Suruí (called "high-tech" Indians by the media)
are trained in information technologies to save their forest.
C. Sombrun, Aquaverde

PART III

The well-behaved daughter raised her son and her half-brother (whose mother was the rebellious daughter). When the boy grew to be a man, the well-behaved daughter thought that it was time to tell him the truth: that the Jaguar Woman, his grandmother, had eaten his mother. He was very angry and made a bow and some arrows and invited the old woman to take a walk with him. Once they were in the forest, he positioned himself behind her to shoot her. But the arrow bounced off without hurting her at all. So he cut down a big tree so that it would fall on her. But the tree did not hurt her. After several attempts, the boy went back to his adoptive mother's house, the well-behaved daughter, and explained that he had not been able to kill his grandmother. "I know that the Jaguar Woman is very afraid of fire," she told him. "I am certain that that would kill her."

So the boy went to get his half-brother and together they invited their grandmother to come fertilize a field by setting it on fire. Once the fire was lit, they gave her a branch.

"Go and throw it in the blaze, grandmother." But when she drew near to it, the boys pushed her and she perished in the flames.

In order to avoid the rage of their father, the son of the Jaguar Woman, they quickly fled. At that time, the earth and the sky were very close together. A bridge existed to go from one to the other. The two young boys took this bridge and destroyed it behind them. That is why the sky is out of reach.

When the Jaguar Woman's son arrived at the blaze, he discovered her body burned to ashes. He blew on her to revive her, but mosquitoes and insects crawled out of her stomach. This is how mosquitoes and insects were created. Her son grew desperate and started to cry.

"Why are you crying?" the river asked.

"Because my sons have killed my mother!"

"I will comfort you," the river answered. "Come to me."

And the Jaguar became the spirit of the river.

And his two sons who went off into the sky became spirits as well.

THE SURUÍ CARBON PROJECT

Now I must tell you about what I think has been the most important accomplishment of our tribe: the Suruí carbon project.

To give you some background, the foundations for the carbon market were laid as a part of the Kyoto protocol when it was decided in 1997 that between 2008 and 2012, the level of global greenhouse gas emissions needed to be reduced to 5.2% of what it was in 1990. The goals of the REDD mechanism (Reducing Emissions from Deforestation and forest Degradation) were further developed during the United Nations Climate Change Conference in Bali in [sic] 2007. The REDD mechanism would provide financial compensation to those who could commit to reducing greenhouse emissions.

I learned about this mechanism thanks to my friend Beto Borges, with whom I reconnected when I was evacuated to California in 2007. We had met at the Centro de Pesquisa Indigena (Center of Indigenous Research)—which was founded by Ailton Krenak—while I was studying at the university. Beto Borges was writing his thesis on Suruí efforts to develop a sustainable agriculture program. In 2007, Borges joined the non-profit organization Forest Trends, where he directed the program that was responsible for promoting local community initiatives and private sector markets. I thought that Forest Trends was like the Aquaverde association and that it could finance our reforestation projects. Beto explained that this was not the case. Forest Trends, among other organizations, was itself seeking funds to finance REDD+ projects[1]. I didn't see then how REDD+ projects could be useful to us, so Beto explained that the trees on our land were potentially the kind of trees that could absorb greenhouse gases.

1: The REDD concept was expanded to REDD+ to take into account the enhancement of forest carbon generated by adapted silviculture practices and plantings that happen in partnership with indigenous peoples and their communities who depend on the forest. The concept still involves remunerating developing countries with contributions from industrialized countries (source: United Nations).

By generating carbon credits, we could very well imagine being remunerated for protecting our forest. But how would we go about it? I asked. Beto explained patiently that there were actually two methods to generate these credits. One was called A/R (afforestation/reforestation) which involved planting trees, and the second one, REDD+, involved preserving an endangered forest.

My children, you can imagine my joy upon hearing this! It was as though a dream were coming true. Thanks to this system, our income would be based on the results of our work and not solely on philanthropy—which is of course certainly laudable—but that makes us totally dependent on state or non-governmental organizations and puts us under their administrative supervision. Additionally, our people would become participants in an ecosystem responding to a real need for carbon capture.

Bolstered by this information, I envisioned developing a REDD+ project on our territory's 248,000 hectares (957 square miles). No tribe had yet attempted such a venture, and this pioneer project, whose basic idea was to finance reforestation and the maintenance of a forest with carbon credits, was still an unattainable dream for us. Nevertheless, I decided to make it our goal. With that money, Indians who did not have other sources of income would no longer be tempted to make deals with the madeireiros or to rent their land for livestock farming or coffee harvesting. Under an official carbon contract, our trees would be better protected from illegal logging. And lastly, a part of the money spent on preserving our forest could be invested into a sustainable development plan that would guarantee our population's survival for at least the next fifty years.

Representatives from ACT and Kanindé helped me gather support from the many branches of our tribe (they spent several months canvassing our villages and explaining the concept). After this, the first step was to answer this central question: could Indians legally own the rights for carbon capture on their land?

Forest Trends helped us once again by commissioning the Baker and McKenzie law firm to do a study. The results were clear. According to their legal opinion, the Brazilian law and constitution did indeed guarantee us the administration and exclusive use of our resources. Additionally, the profits would belong to us. This was very good news because although we knew that their legal opinion was not the letter of the law, their opinion could influence the judicial system, and we were hoping it would set a precedent that would be applied to all of Brazil and then to other countries.

Thus we were able to say that our rights to the carbon credits that our forest would produce were a means toward our sustainable development project. And that the connection between our territories and carbon credits was indeed a way of securing our financial future—that our putting the sustainable development projects in place could ensure our survival without destroying our forests or the biodiversity of our forest.

From here, our Suruí Carbon Project was able to get off the ground.

I decided to contact several organizations in order to give our project every possible chance of success: the best ones in each of the domains that we would be learning more about.

"So you're assembling a whole consortium for this project!" my friend Beto said, laughing.

I told him that a single organization could do this work, but if we asked an organization to do it, wouldn't we then be at risk once again of being dependent on an organization? I suggested that we continue working with ACT and Kanindé and that Beto develop contacts at IDESAM (the Institute for the Conservation and Sustainable Development of the Amazon) and at Katoomba Incubator, an initiative of the Forest Trends organization that was working to support innovative projects that could be reproduced all over the world.

While on a trip to Europe where I had been invited for protest events promoting indigenous people's rights, I was able to meet the leaders of the Alternative Carbon organization. Their technical teams, along with our different specialists committed to the project, were able to start working on the key methodological questions and baseline scenario questions.

Next we had to do an evaluation of our forest's potential. Given that we had decided to develop a REDD+ project of preserving an endangered forest, we had to determine which of our land parcels were the most at risk. The technicians of IDESAM did the evaluation and a biomass survey developed using an internationally recognized methodology.

Next, it was established that over the next thirty years, 13,500 hectares (52 square miles) of our forest were endangered and therefore at risk of being transformed into farmland. Losing this forest corresponded to nearly 8 million tons of carbon dioxide

emissions. However, preserving the trees would mean avoiding more than 90% of deforestation and would "compensate" for the equivalent of 5 million tons of carbon credits, or 170,000 tons per year between 2010 and 2040.

To give you an idea, one carbon credit amounts to permission granting the right to emit up to one ton of carbon equivalent. The price of the credits varies quite a bit, but even when we ran a pessimistic evaluation with the price at just four dollars per credit, we determined that if a business wanted to buy Suruí carbon credits to compensate for 5 million tons of carbon emissions that we were capable of producing over the next 30 years, that business would pay us 20 million dollars. This is quite a sum, of course, and yet we didn't want to accept doing business with just anyone. That is why we decided to impose our own carbon management system in which we would refuse to sell our credits to any business that would not commit to reducing their harmful emissions or would not heed our recommendations for figuring out how do it. The reasoning behind this was to make sure that each party's responsibilities were well-defined.

Despite all of this potential, I was well aware that our Mother Earth was not supposed to follow the rules of the economic markets and that the REDD+ project was not going to be a perfect solution. It actually created the opportunities for much abuse, which I will explain later. But even if our Suruí carbon project wasn't perfect, it was nevertheless going to contribute to an awakening of consciences by demonstrating it was possible to generate profits from the rainforest without destroying it!

And that is exactly what our project did. The international press—*Der Spiegel, The Independent, National Geographic, Smithsonian, The Washington Post, Life, Época,* CNN, *San Francisco Chronicle, La Tribune de Genève, Das Magazin* and *Géo*—ran huge headlines about it: the Suruí carbon project will soon make the "High-tech Indians" the first indigenous people to be paid for preserving their forest!

The last thing we needed to do was get our project approved on the independent carbon market and to get the certification that we needed. This was by no means the simplest part of this challenge, but the recognition from the press gave me strength. Our people were finally being taken seriously, and several famous personalities, including Prince Charles and artists such as Brazilian musician José Barrense-Dias, French actress Agnès Soral and Grace Young, singer of the American group Grace and the Victory Riders (who would become patrons of the Aquaverde association), started advocating for

our cause. In 2008, I was very surprised to receive the Human Rights Award from the International Service of Human Rights in Geneva in recognition for my commitment and peaceful and proactive fight for my people and our environment, as well as for my role as a spokesperson for numerous indigenous organizations in Latin America. And then in 2009, the Brazilian magazine *Época* named me one of the 100 most important personalities in Brazil!

"Father, you are the best!" my children told me.

I was proud, of course. Earning the respect of one's children is the most beautiful thing that a father could hope for, right? I must confess that when I am dead, I would indeed like it if wherever my children go, they are told their father was well-respected. But I recall what I told my kids when they said I was the best: I said something my father once said to me: "Never go into a fight thinking that you are the best. And if you're told that you are, get to work right away on behalf of other people."

So, I went back to join my clan and got back to work. We had to put a particularly important aspect of our sustainable management plan for our forest resources in place: biomonitoring.

Biomonitoring meant first doing a systematic survey of the animal species with whom we were sharing the land. For example, when we went out to hunt peccary, we took photos and counted them. We sent this information directly to the database belonging to a biologist from the Kanindé Ethno-Environmental Protection Association who would then tell us what species were endangered. Then it was up to us to restrict our hunting, increase it, or ban it altogether.

We also had to determine if we should continue breeding cattle or not. We learned how to breed cattle from the settlers after contact, but we quickly noticed that it came along with two major problems: it required a lot of deforestation and it was not very profitable. Our family tradition dictates that we are not allowed to kill our domestic animals, cows or chickens, which was forcing us to sell them to a slaughterhouse and then buy back the meat. So, we decided to stop raising livestock and instead prioritize protecting the forest and agroforestry.

In 2009, we began reflecting on the 40 years that had gone by since contact: what had

we gained? What had we lost? How could we move forward?

The answer to the first two questions lies in what I have just explained. To answer the last question, we decided that we needed to further develop our 50-year plan. For example, we could make it more effective if we improved the democratic structure among our people. To do this we decided to reinstate our traditional governance structures and start reconstructing our internal political system with the help of the various perspectives within our tribe.

After a year of discussions, it was decided that the Paiter Suruí would be led by a council composed of the twelve oldest members of the tribe, that is, three from each of the four clans. This parliament would elect the chief of the Suruí, and the community would elect the chief of each village (aldeia).

This new, more democratic system was voted into effect in 2010, the year that I was elected *labiway esage,* the chief of the Paiter Suruí. Our council endeavored to write a code that included our socio-historic-cultural characteristics and defined the big picture for the future development of our education, the environment, the sustainable management of our resources, our institutional development, our governance system, our religious practices, etc.

As we encountered problems we refined the Suruí code. It is now the framework in which we organize our struggle for sustainable development. Soon the Suruí code will be taught in our schools since we realized that our young people study Brazilian and European history but do not study much of our own. Indigenous teachers appointed by the Municipal School of Cacoal can now receive specific university training in Mato Grosso and they can teach classes in Portuguese as well as in Tupi-monde. In 2000, a master's degree was created for students wanting to specialize in natural sciences, social sciences or languages.

THE "HIGH-TECH INDIANS"

2011 marked the arrival of Confúcio Moura as the governor of our state of Rondônia. Moura quickly demonstrated his willingness to reestablish a dialogue with Indian leaders that finally allowed us to share our point of view: that the State of Rondônia was one of the most violently affected by deforestation: 40% of its rainforest had already been destroyed for livestock farming and agricultural development. Would our Suruí territory suffer the same fate?

Of course, some of our people were able to make deals with the loggers, but the moratorium on this activity had been upheld. Indeed, for three years, funds from the organizations helping us to develop our Suruí Carbon Project had allowed us to meet our basic needs. The harmful logging that was still happening was due exclusively to timber poaching, and despite our surveillance, 5% of our forest (12,000 hectares) had been illegally destroyed. If the State of Rondônia had not been helping us to stop the madeireiros who were responsible for it, we would have lost 30% of the rainforest's surface area in less than 50 years—like the other tribes, since because it was impossible to monitor the entire expanse of our territories, these people were free to plunder them without punishment.

Admittedly, the loggers' methods were smart. In the name of "land occupation," they started by deforesting a "front" ranging from a few dozen to several hundreds of kilometers. The money from selling the timber then allowed them to open access roads, grow grass, buy cattle and have it graze on the land, and then later resell it. Simply put, it was pure profit. Confúcio Moura reminded us that the federal government had started a surveillance system of the Amazon rainforest in 1992 called SIVAM to halt illegal deforestation and clearing of the rainforest by burning it. A governmental department called SIPAM

(Amazonian Protection Service) replaced and continued the surveillance in 2002. A billion dollars was then invested in a surveillance and grid system for the Amazonian territories using satellite and radar aircraft. This technology was supposed to be able to pass through cloud layers that covered the tree canopy more than seven months of the year and it was able to map out little by little what we call the Amazonian demographic "vacuum": an unexplored territory of about 2 million square kilometers (772,204 square miles)—nearly three times the surface area of France. A scan using a six-meter ground resolution uncovered an Amazon rainforest heretofore unknown. It revealed the rainforest's geological diversity and its subsoil, and also allowed us to detect deforestation in real time. Once evidence of deforestation had been detected, IBAMA (the Brazilian Institute of the Environment and Renewable Natural Resources) was alerted, which then triggered an intervention by a surveillance team.

I must mention that at that time, President Lula da Silva's government had made an effort to better implement a protective measure for the rainforest that had been written in 1965 but little-respected since: the Brazilian Forest Code. It was deemed one of the most rigorous forest codes in the world, mandating that each farmer preserve 80% of rainforest on their land. The strictest implementation of this code has slowed deforestation since 2004, decreasing it by more than 10,000 square kilometers (3,861 square miles).

Marina Silva, Lula's Environment Minister at the time, helped to a large degree as well. Born into a poor family from a community of seringueiros (rubber harvesters) in the State of Acre, she had always fought for the preservation of the rainforest, most notably alongside Chico Mendes. She was appointed in 2003 by President Lula and backed the implementation of a national plan for the fight against deforestation by creating protected zones for indigenous populations and later by coordinating the efforts of the police, the army and the IBAMA departments. In a country where 80% of the wood production resulted from timber poaching, she also initiated hundreds of operations to arrest those responsible and dismantled more than 1,500 illegal businesses.

Marina Silva resigned in 2008 in opposition to plans for energy development, agro fuels and genetically modified crops, which were all a part of the policy supported by Dilma Rousseff, who was at that time Lula's Chief of Staff. Silva's efforts did result, however, in the deforestation rate finally dropping in 2010.

But it was still impossible for the tribes to control the entirety of their territories. To

help with this, starting in 2009, Google Earth Outreach sent some employees to teach us how to use the Open Data Kit system. Photos and videos from Android mobile phones are geo-tagged by GPS to flag instances of timber poaching, and then the images are uploaded in real time into Google Maps Engine mapping tools. Although, Google Earth Outreach alone was not enough to stop the pillaging of our trees, it nonetheless allowed us to show the scope of the deforestation in our area. Broadcasting photos and videos on YouTube helped convince Governor Moura how essential it was for him to help us.

Having three environmental police agents permanently assigned to our territory led to 15 illegal sawmills being closed and, for the first time since contact, the virtual disappearance of timber poaching. This was certainly a tremendous victory but I was not able to celebrate for long . . .

A new bounty of $100,000 had been put on my head.

I would certainly be lying, of course, if I said that I was not discouraged by this. But do you know who gave me the strength to go on? Dikimuya, our oldest warrior at 106 years old, my grandfather's last living friend.

"Almir, my boy, soon I am going to die and I want to thank you for your work to save our rainforest. Your grandfather Yabnabi and I often walked beneath these trees. He died before contact and you never knew him, but I know your father told you his story. I know that he must have taught you many things about how to lead our tribe. He was a good chief, as you know, and was also a great warrior. Now I can leave this world in peace and I want to tell you this: the first thing that I will do in the other world will be to go and tell your grandfather how you fulfilled his last wish."

Dikimuya never knew to what extent I needed to hear his words. He joined the Gorakoy a few hours later. In the event that I leave to join him too soon, I want to tell my children now that his last wish is also mine. I want our rainforest to be preserved for them to build a better future. This is what gives me the strength to continue this struggle.

THE PAMINE PROJECT

For a long time I've thought about how to increase the impact of the sustainable management plan that we created for the rainforest. It felt important to do, but I wasn't happy with any of the solutions that had been put forward: we could advertise it, make YouTube videos about it, hold conferences or symposia about it. But then that tropical rainstorm gave me an idea . . .

As is often the case, we were meeting in the big maloca, a huge straw hut without walls where we would gather to share food and simply talk, or lie in hammocks that hooked to the many beams that supported the roof. On that particular day, I was rocking gently in a hammock watching the rain soak into the ground. Small streams were forming in the hollows in the dirt that only the water seemed to notice. I watched as they overflowed the hollows and formed other streams, and then more and more. And then even more beyond that. Right at that moment, something Marimop said popped into my mind as clear as a bell. How could I have forgotten it?

"Changing mindsets and raising awareness begins with setting an example."

I may have even let out a triumphant cry at that moment. If our plan proved efficient, others would want to use it, and then more, and then even more, until the rainforest was saved at last.

Thus, the Pamine Project was born. We named it this since Pamine means "rebirth" in Tupi-monde.

The goal of the Pamine Project was to make our 50-year plan available to the 180 Amazonian tribes in Brazil that had already been contacted. Together they possess 25% of the rainforest, and if each tribe used this model effectively as a tool that was tried and tested by the Suruí , together we could manage to save around 300,000 square kilometers

(74,131,614 acres) of the largest tropical rainforest in the world, that is, nearly half of the surface area of France.

Today, nearly 50 of these tribes have already adopted our model to chart out their ways of life and their development strategies, but I hope to quickly convince the majority of them. As for the 67 tribes that have yet to be contacted (60 according to the FUNAI), we have decided to leave them in peace.

For the most part, these isolated tribes are located in the states of Mato Grosso, Maranhão and here in Rondônia. For the record, I must say that their desire to not establish contact is not for ideological reasons but rather because their memory of prior contacts and their consequences remain painful to this day. The atrocities committed against their ancestors in the 1920s by gold miners, farmers, rubber harvesters and loggers, who were quick to enslave them or to hunt them like game drove these people into hiding and refusing any further contact. I know that the territories of several of these isolated Indian groups (I estimate 300 in Rondônia) are near Porto Velho, near the hydroelectric dams in Jirau and Santo Antônio, on the Madeira River. They've been frightened by the noise from the stopes where the mining occurs, they've been poisoned by the mercury used in gold extraction, and they've seen their territories eaten away by deforestation. They have been forced to abandon their land to go and hide deeper and deeper inside the rainforest.

I was a part of an international activist organization fighting to give these isolated Indian groups the choice of whether to make contact or not. Since 1987, the FUNAI has had a department dedicated to them. Their policy is to establish contact only in the event of an extreme emergency (that would endanger their survival) and to protect them by attempting to obtain official demarcation of their territories. I can't help but tell you here about the example of the Indian nicknamed "the Man of the Hole." He is the only remaining survivor of his tribe, which was most likely massacred by farmers. Since then, he has continued digging holes to hide in. The territory that the FUNAI assigned him is located right next to our neighbors the Gavião, but nothing could be done to prevent this man from being gradually surrounded by livestock farms. In 2009, he was the victim of an armed assault. Shots were fired by local farmers opposed to the efforts of the FUNAI to protect him and opposed to his presence on the middle of their land, but the investigation resulted in not a single arrest. But do not worry, despite

everything, the "Man of the Hole" survived the assault and continues to live off his small piece of land while still refusing all contact. Yet the question remains as to whether he and all others in his situation will be left in peace for much longer.

The implementation of the PAC (Growth Acceleration Program) introduced by the second Lula government (2006-2010) does not make us very hopeful. Under the pretext of building roads necessary for the Growth Acceleration Program, the government began a campaign to contact the Indians who were in voluntarily isolation. We think this was one way of getting their permission to set up infrastructures such as hydroelectric dams, which would supposedly meet the electricity needs of an "exponentially growing country." But despite official communications arguing that millions of people would potentially benefit from the new power-generation capacity, here we all know that the electricity will instead be sold to other countries, as Paraguay has done. We also know that these dams are designed to serve the needs of mining industries, notably for bauxite extraction from the deposits in Pará, and that completing the dams—in addition to allowing access to the resources in the subsoil upon which they were built—will make Brazil the second largest producer of hydro-electric power in the world after China.

To get back to our tribe, I would say that without any legal means of fighting these governmental decisions, our only weapon was, once again, to increase awareness and to try to change people's mindsets with realistic solutions.

So, we planned to strengthen our 50-year plan and make it more efficient by developing a partnership with the Federal University of Rondônia as well as with their campus in Cacoal. The formal partnerships are in process, but as soon as they are in effect, the students of the school of biology will grow seedlings that we will then replant in the rainforest. In the meantime, representatives of our Metareilá association have received permission to organize seminars. Once a year, they provide students with an active learning experience with environmental issues by giving them a small tree that they are then responsible for planting. We gave out 500 last year. The trees are right there in front of their eyes that they care for as they grow and get taller. This is a good start. They provide a concrete example that reminds the students every day of their duty to protect them.

Do you know who gave me this idea? The moon. That evening, the blue light of the

moon had flooded the forest. I watched it for a while, fascinated, its pastel color as soft as the *jinipapo* pigment that we use for our body paint. The image of my father hunting tatou reminded me of the legend that I was told when I turned eleven years old. Let it be said that this was a time when I was no longer completely uninterested in girls...

"The moon has not always existed, you know," my father said.

I raised my eyebrows.

"But after the story I am about to tell you, you will never look at it the same way again!"

One day, a family from the half of our people that works in the fields (the iwai), was very busy preparing the chicha, the drink we offer to the other half that works in the forest (the metareda) during Mapimaï. In this particular family, there were two brothers and two sisters. One of the daughters was named Akapeab and she was very beautiful. She was in seclusion since she had just had her first period and was to be married to her maternal uncle at the end of this period. As is the tradition, he was a part of the forest half and had moved into the metareilá, the clearing in which the forest half lived while they prepared for the festival. He built bows and other gifts that the members of his group would offer to the other group.

One night, a man entered into Akapeab's hut. It was a very dark night—the moon did not yet exist—and he lay down in her hammock. Very softly she asked him, "Is it you, maternal uncle, doing this to me?"

"Yes, it's me, your maternal uncle."

He came back the next night and the young woman asked him again, "Is it you, maternal uncle?"

"Yes, it's me. But do not tell anyone that I come here each night."

She was intrigued by his request and the young woman wondered whether this man was truly her uncle. When he came the next night, she asked him again, "Is it you, uncle?"

"Yes, it's me!"

So, she threw a bit of of jenipapo pigment on his face, the same pigment that we use to draw our ritual body paintings. He thought this was strange, but the young woman told him it was water.

The next day, she told her mother what had happened. "Mother, is it really my uncle who is coming to see me each night?"

"No, it can't be. An uncle would never do that to his niece before the seclusion period is over! Did you ask him if he was really your uncle?"

"Of course, I did. He said he was, but he said not to tell anyone!"

"Why would he want to keep it a secret? If he were your uncle, he would know that you are his designated bride and he would have waited until you had finished the seclusion period!"

The mother didn't think it could be her brother. So, if it had been another man, like a cousin, the jenipapo that her daughter had thrown that is impossible to wipe off would give him away. So, the mother went to the metareilá and found her brother, but there was not a single trace of pigment on his face. She returned to the village to look at all of the men from the half of the tribe that works the fields (iwai).

When she finished her investigation, she went to see her daughter. "I have very bad news. It was not your uncle who came to see you. His face has no pigment on it. It was your brother. It is his face that bears the marks!"

The young woman was despondent and started to cry. "It's my own brother who has been coming to see me every night!"

The mother cried as well because her daughter had been disgraced. Akapeab ended her seclusion period and left the hut without painting her body or adorning herself with any of the bridal decorations as she would have if she were marrying her uncle. "Mother, kill me with this arrow. I must die!"

"No," her mother replied. "Your brother and you must now go to the sky!"

And so, the brother and sister climbed a liana that reached all the way into the sky. And that is how the moon, which did not exist until then, appeared. The light side of the moon represents the face of Akapeab and the dark side represents her brother's face, still painted with the pigment of jinipapo.

"And that," my father told me, "is how the moon reminds us every night that we must never commit incest."

So, on that particular evening, the idea came to me that each little tree planted by a student from our seminars could continually remind them that they must protect the trees. . . .

A SURUÍ UNIVERSITY, OR WHAT THE FOREST CAN TEACH US

We believed that in order to raise awareness and change people's mindsets, we needed to create a Suruí university that could bring together all of the rainforest's traditional and scientific knowledge. We needed a way to make this knowledge available to all and for us to put that knowledge to use to better protect it. I still believe that this needs to be the contribution of the peoples of the Amazon rainforest. We have been guarding and cultivating the ancestral knowledge of the Amazon rainforest for thousands of years, so we need to draw attention to the tremendous risks of the rainforest possibly disappearing.

Need I remind you that as well as being one of the richest examples of biodiversity in the world, the rainforest is the world's largest freshwater reserve and is a vital source of life that's necessary for maintaining the planet's climate equilibrium? To doom the rainforest would be to condemn entire regions to suffer severe floods and undergo irreversible damage. This would include plants with medicinal properties which live in the rainforest. Only 2% of their active substances—and I do mean only 2%—have been indexed and studied in a lab at this point in time. Is not the other 98% a treasure? Wouldn't it be completely irresponsible to deprive humanity of this wealth? To give you an even more concrete example, I will share two lessons with you that the rainforest has taught me.

As I was confronting new problems each day, I learned how to adapt. I think that this is why our tribe has been able to take on the new lifestyle that was imposed on us in just 40 years. It is thanks to this adaptation that I am as at ease with a bow as I am

with an iPhone, a Twitter account or a Facebook page. My children recently made fun of me for being a "geek" and I agreed with them wholeheartedly! This new technology has given me so much in terms of knowledge about our planet and I am so happy to have been able to adapt to it. But wouldn't it be good for other people to have a turn learning what the forest has taught us?

Here is one example. To cleanse the body, we drink a concoction made of the moratapo liana. We say "renew" in our language because the body purifies itself, whereas the mind renews itself. Isn't this an important realization? Every time I got a fever or a migraine, Peripeira, our *wáwá,* would go to cut a few leaves of a shrub that grows near our houses. If I sprain my ankle, Peripeira grates the branches of the capichanapua bark and applies the sap to my foot. Capichanapua is a powerful analgesic and anti-inflammatory. We also use the slime from snails to soften calluses on our feet. When I have a toothache, all I need to do is simply chew on a stalk of haïn. The tart taste anesthetizes my mouth and heals the infection. A red eye? Our *wáwá* cuts a branch of the ipaga, scrapes and squeezes the bark to extract its juice and then pours it drop by drop into the irritated eye. It clears up immediately! The forest offers us thousands of simple and efficient remedies that our Suruí University would make available to everyone.

I also learned from the rainforest that each tree, flower, and insect has a purpose. The ecosystem serves as a model of equilibrium for our people. We must learn together to behave like one forest in which each individual is necessary, where each root of each plant deserves to be protected for the harmony and good of all. Today people do what their hands tell them to, but they need to understand that their hands don't simply act on their own. There is wisdom behind what they do. We call it *soe same.* If the special features and the roots of each are respected, this wisdom will grow out of all our essences, from all of our minds, and become a common global mind. This is how we will become a beautiful forest.

That, is what our Suruí university could teach others.

To help spread this knowledge, we had the idea to create a cultural center. The blueprints for it have just been drawn up. The center will be located near our village of Lapetanha, and it will offer a biodiversity research space as well as a conference room for seminars on sustainable development. The Suruí university may also generate income which would

further help to secure us financially.

We are still waiting for the government to legally recognize our university, but our work has already received a significant amount of praise. The Metareilá association was named a finalist for Brazil's prize for best social entrepreneur for our work improving living conditions, preserving our cultural heritage and the environment. The American magazine *Fast Company* named me as one of the world's 100 Most Creative People in Business, and I was also named Commander of the Brazilian National Order of Cultural Merit. I even received the Cacau de ouro (Golden Cocoa Bean), an award given annually by the Brazilian newspaper Diário da Amazônia to deserving citizens of Rondônia. I was out of the country on the day the award was given, so I asked my children to accept the award in my place. This was because had it not been with their help, I would have probably given up. I was therefore very happy to learn how moved they were to hold the Cacau de ouro in their hands when they went to the ceremony and accepted it for me.

ACCOLADES AND
MORE DEATH THREATS

The year 2012 marked an important milestone for the sustainable management of the rainforest. It was not just a milestone, but a real victory because in June, our Suruí carbon project was finally accepted onto the independent carbon market with two international certifications: the CCB standard (Climate, Community and Biodiversity), committing us to preserving our rainforest by conserving its biodiversity; and the VCS standard (Verified Carbon Standard), obtained after the amount of deforestation (carbon REDD+) that we were able to avoid between 2009 and 2012 was determined. This may seem very complicated, but simply put, this was proof that, if not for the income from carbon credits, the Suruí would indeed have had to cut down a part of their rainforest in order to survive.

But we still had to begin the auditing phase. This is the most critical phase since it involves an audit that determines whether our land meets the criteria required for putting our carbon credits on the independent carbon market.

The audit was conducted by representatives of the Institute of Agricultural and Forest Management and Certification (IMAFLORA), the American non-governmental organization Rainforest Alliance, and the Institute for Conservation and Sustainable Development of Amazonas (IDESAM), the group responsible for conducting a satellite image analysis of our land. It goes without saying that we were very impatient to find out the results of the audit. Years of work and hope for the survival of our forest and of our trip depended on it.

We got the response in May 2013—I will come back to this later. At first, all that this recognition of our management policy did for the forest was to prompt the madeireiros to renew their death threats against me: they took out another contract for $100,000 on my head. I expected as much, but this time I alerted the United Nations Commission on Human Rights in New York, which forced the Brazilian government to open an investigation.

The human rights commission of the Brazilian government immediately provided me with physical protection that involved a rotation of six body guards, all Brazilian federal agents, as well as a driver, all of whose contracts were renewed every three months in response to local investigations. Only seven other people in Brazil were at that time benefitting from that level of protection, two of whom were federal judges and five were environmentalists. Of the seven, I am the only Indian. This seems unfortunately far from adequate because the problem of deforestation and large-scale economic development in the Amazon rainforest has been resurfacing with new urgency.

Because of this, numerous conservationists in Rondônia are in danger. In May of 2011, Adelino Ramos, an activist with the Corumbiara Peasant Movement, was shot in Vista Alegre do Abunã. Three others were assassinated in the State of Pará, in all likelihood killed by hitmen. Each one of them had condemned timber poaching and had been threatened before, but it must also be said that these murders took place after Congress adopted amendments to the laws protecting Brazilian rainforests (which I will come back to later) which seem to have been perceived as a weakening of environmental regulations currently in place. The local NGOs had warned that these changes came with the risk of inciting more violence on the part of the livestock farmers and those involved in timber poaching, but the government proceeded anyway.

To address this issue of the death threats, the federal government put an interdepartmental task force in place that was responsible for looking into a list of 25 people who had been threatened. Would this actually help prevent further assassinations? Not likely, since measures also needed to be taken to deal with perpetrators going unpunished and to address the continual lawlessness of the situation. Indeed, according to the Pastoral Land Commission (CPT), out of the 1,800 conservationists that had received death threats over the last ten years, more than 100 had been killed between 2010 and 2011 alone, without any of the killers ever being arrested. The authorities therefore—notably

the Brazilian Institute of the Environment and Renewable Natural Resources (IBAMA) and the state's public safety services—need to share their information and investigate the threats being made on our lives. If this does not happen, my body guards won't be able to protect me for very long.

I must admit, it is all becoming a heavier and heavier burden to carry. It becomes even more so when I see flashes of fear in the eyes of my wives and my children. They nevertheless have acted with dignity and have never begrudged me for imposing this burden on them. I want to tell them how much I admire them for this. Certainly, the great forest taught them that a tree must sometimes sacrifice itself for the other ones, but I am proud to see they have learned from this wisdom how not to be self-centered, to love their neighbors, and to recognize the value of our culture. This knowledge is theirs. No one can take it away from them, and I am happy to have helped transmit that knowledge to them. I know very well that one day it will be their turn to do the same and that it will be a heavy responsibility, but I know that they will put all of their hearts and souls into it. My children understand this well: that love is the only resource from which you should draw your strength.

The day I was elected chief of the Suruí people in 2010, the *wáwá* came to see me to tell me that the spirit of our tribe had spoken to him in the night: my name from then on would be Narayamoga, "the spirit uniting spiritual powers" and I would be a leader in the charge against great struggles throughout the world.

"But your greatest challenge," the *wáwá* said, "will be your own people. If you love them enough to understand them, then you will be a great leader. If not, you will not conquer this challenge."

This scared me quite a bit. But I knew that he was right about at least one thing: being a leader would not be easy. Therefore, I have always taken the time to sit down and speak with the people in my tribe. Nevertheless, I still am under many kinds of pressures and recently—I am not ashamed to say it—I wanted to give up.

Since 2011, we have noticed that timber poaching on our land has resumed. We did what we could to limit it and always tried to do this non-violently; those of us who came across a truck loaded with wood would simply make the driver climb down out of the truck and tell him to return on foot. But, for a few months now, the deforestation has

increased and by our calculations, forty trucks filled with wood were leaving our land in secret each day. Forty truckloads of timber! And what could we do? Nothing. Because the government still was not giving us any legal leverage to stop them. And the worst part was realizing that what was being stolen from us had the potential to jeopardize our entire carbon project. Our carbon credits were in the process of being audited and we were being rated on how much deforestation we were preventing. Would the credits still be approved if we weren't able to avoid deforestation? This would mean years of work and struggle for absolutely nothing. Nothing.

THE RESULTS

The long-awaited result of the audit which would determine whether or not our territory met the criteria for putting our carbon credits on the independent carbon market came in May 2013. Was our project approved or not? I will let you find out by reading the answer, as I did when I opened the letter: "The result of the audits show that the Suruí have reduced the equivalent of 250,000 tons of carbon emissions between 2009 and 2012." I read this and immediately let out a shout of victory. I turned to kiss the person closest to me at that moment—it was Sergente, my bodyguard. He certainly wasn't expecting it, but the news seemed to make him happy. (At that point, we were spending most of our time together, like twins!)

Putting our carbon credits on the market brought back some doubts that I had mostly pushed aside for months: who would want to buy Suruí carbon credits?

Fortunately, we did not have to wait long to be approached by potential buyers. I should mention that our goal was to prioritize selling our credits to Brazilian companies. This was a political strategy to counter our critics who claimed that we were willing to turn our land over to outsiders. While I'm on the topic of our critics, I now want to explain the wrongdoing that resulted from our involvement with the REDD+ program.

When unscrupulous organizations realized the potential of the profits from the carbon market, some of them proposed that we give up the right to manage our carbon credits so that they could sell them for us. Clearly, we refused, but I know that these organizations have used their persuasive powers to convince nearly twenty tribes to give over their control. The tribes quickly realized that their contracts with these organizations even prohibited them from using their own land. And even though the government nullified their contracts, and our carbon initiative is the only one currently recognized, these tribes will have to undergo lengthy legal procedures to be able to manage their

own resources again.

Other critics claimed that the REDD+ program was "the commodification of Nature." I can't say that it isn't, but I must ask: have these people proposed any other solutions that would generate profits from the forest without destroying it? They haven't. And meanwhile, our Suruí carbon credits project has become the first commercialized indigenous project to comply with the legal requirements of the international market as well as with the standards set up in policies protecting indigenous rights. This is a precedent that I hope will encourage many other indigenous groups to adopt our model. While it is not ideal, the REDD+ mechanism is at least able to provide some leverage which forces the capitalist system to acknowledge the value of a sustainably managed rainforest. And not just that, but also the fact that the REDD+ mechanism is a way to financially support indigenous people while at the same time they are protecting their environment and culture.

TACKLING THE REFORESTATION PROBLEM

And then there occurred an incident among our own people.

My brother Mopiri called me one morning. I was in Geneva with Thomas Pizer working to convince an international organization to support our cause. When I answered the phone, Mopiri exploded in anger. He had just heard that the Indians from line 14 were harshly criticizing my approach. I told my brother to calm down. I had made mistakes and perhaps they were right. Mopiri quickly cut me off and told me he learned that despite my instructions and the moratorium that the ensemble of our chiefs had agreed to, some chiefs were secretly selling to timber poachers.

Naturally, I was quite upset. But I knew that in exchange for exploiting the resources of our land, the timber poachers were continuing to offer money or other everyday consumer products—building materials, televisions or even refrigerators—which were still prohibitively expensive by our standard of living. It was no excuse, but I understood very well how some among us were giving in to temptation. Putting the interests of the group before one's own is not easy, as you know. And it's even harder when it prevents you from achieving your dreams.

So, I told my brother that I would sit down with them again to try to convince them that a short-term, profit-directed approach would very quickly leave us without any resources at all—and with no other way to generate carbon credits. What future could we offer our children then? Mopiri told me he had even worse news. I held my breath.

"The same people are saying that you are using our cause to enjoy yourself while you travel the world."

I gritted my teeth at the brutal shock of this news, but I let him go on.

"They also are saying that they will stop selling our timber once you step down as chief."

As violently as a gust of wind puts out a fire, I felt a tremendous sadness extinguish my morale. I told Mopiri that I was going to give up. If these Indians truly thought that it would be easy for them to work with organizations that we had spent years persuading to support us, let them try. In the end, they would realize that building a relationship of trust does not happen overnight. They would understand how exhausting the role of a leader is. How terrifying. How thankless. And that, fair or not, a leader's actions are always harshly criticized: the same Indians had gone so far as to start a rumor that fighting for this cause was somehow making me lots of money. But they are well aware that when I return home the electricity gets cut off since I cannot pay the bills, that people are threatening to cut my head off, too, for supporting our cause, and that I live with bodyguards twenty-four hours of every day. How absurd and unfair!

Very suddenly I felt an urgent need to talk to my father, to tell him how much I missed him. Marimop had always guided me in moments of doubt. I looked up to the sky to address him. It was silly, it's true, but perhaps I did it to remember how I used to look up at him when I was a child.

"What would you do in my place, Bà?"

Was this struggle worth all of this sacrifice? Did it justify my implicating my family, my friends, and all of my people who still trusted me? I lowered my head. What have I brought my children, other than the fear of seeing me assassinated? I haven't even brought them better schools. Was I making a huge mistake?

When I went back to Lapetanha, I sat down alongside my clan members. One of them told me:

"You know, Almir, I was with your father when he was dying. He wanted you to be strong, to act without believing you would win with no effort, to act without thinking that you wouldn't make any mistakes. Your mistakes are far fewer than the contributions that you have made. Believe me, a much larger struggle awaits you. The majority of the Suruí are still counting on you to tackle the reforestation problem!"

His words encouraged me. I was taken back into the moment when my father and I were hunting in the forest, just a few months before his final departure . . .

We were tracking a peccary when, all of a sudden, we were caught in the rain—a tropical rain that drenched our clothes in less than ten seconds. Marimop didn't seek out shelter. He calmly tore off a long paraah leaf. He rubbed it gently between his hands to extract a slimy green juice and applied it to his head and laughed.

"There's nothing like a good rain for washing your hair!"

I followed suit. The paraah is a natural shampoo, one of our forest's treasures that I realized I hadn't used in a long time.

"You know," he added as the rain streamed through our hair, "the great Amazon rainforest has already lost twenty-five percent of its surface area."

I nodded sadly. I knew that at this rate, it was predicted that the rainforest would be completely destroyed before the end of the 21st century. Since the forest absorbs carbon dioxide from the atmosphere, it is a key player in confronting the challenge of global warming. How would our children recover from this? Why were governments content to simply manage our resources only over the short term? Would wisdom never conquer over greed? As though he had heard my exact thoughts, Marimop looked me straight in the eye.

"Soon I will no longer be here to walk alongside you in this struggle. But hear what I say, my son. Never be discouraged, for all those people destroying our trees will one day come to us to buy our tree seedlings and beg us to teach them the wisdom of the forest!"

I resumed the struggle.

We, the Suruí, had been successful in preserving 95% of our rainforest. We had to keep going. We had to set an example. And we had to raise awareness and change people's mindsets without waiting for the government to help. Can I share a little secret? To give myself strength and restore my courage, I did then what I always do: I watched soccer games and cheered on Brazil's team. I listened to Raul Seixas, the father of Brazilian rock. My children always say he's crazy, but when I am with Seixas I feel less alone.

Good news arrived shortly thereafter.

The Federal Institute of Education of Rondônia signed a cooperation agreement for our Suruí university project and it didn't stop there. We were also in negotiations with the national university to establish a partnership that would educate students about our rainforest resource management policy. With this partnership, everyone would have

access to our knowledge.

Though nothing has been finalized yet, I began discussions with the town leaders of Cacoal about changes that need to be made at the municipal level, such as encouraging farmers to expand organic crops and convincing cattle farmers to introduce a quality certification process that farmers could obtain once they committed to running their farms without deforestation. This would be a responsible and respectful approach towards development. The mayor is not yet ready, but we have already obtained ample support, thanks to which I was able to meet sixty leaders of the Rondônia farming organizations in June of 2013. I spoke with them, of course, about our idea of creating "green" or sustainable municipalities. Here again, in order to raise awareness and change mindsets, we must provide examples of how to do it. So, I asked the president of the organization of a municipality in the State of Pará who was already successfully practicing this kind of farming to accompany me. From here, we will need to meet with breeders' associations. I hope that they will hear our message!

THE HUMMINGBIRD

The last element of our project, but not the least, is obtaining complete financial autonomy. Putting our Suruí carbon credits on the market was an important step. In August 2013, Natura Cosméticos, the leading Brazilian cosmetics retailer, bought the equivalent of 120,000 tons of carbon offset credits from us. They have committed to reducing their greenhouse gas emissions before the end of 2013 to one third the level of the emissions in 2006. The transaction with Natura Cosméticos was the first of its kind and I know that there are now other tribes of the Amazon who have decided to follow our example. Believe me when I say that we celebrated this historic moment!

But we also wanted to think about ways to develop and monetize our handicrafts, such as the necklaces made from tucumã seeds, wicker baskets, belts and black ceramic pots, small gourds with one or two spouts. Additionally, the sales and the production of Brazil nuts, bananas, pupunha, cocoa or fruits of the açaï palm that we use to make very delicious ice creams—we make these products ourselves, of course, with no impact on biodiversity.

Historically, each family had its own field, and once the harvest was over, we would move and create another village with other crops. It was a way to not tire out the land, as I have mentioned before. Now the State gives us food staples (salt, corn, rice, small amounts of oil), and the villages no longer relocate. However, it is still the community that decides where each person will plant their crops. Fields of light feeding crops, such as manioc (cassava), are relocated after each harvest, whereas fields where we plant banana trees and coffee trees are only moved every five years.

We are also planning to create a mobile sawmill in order to use the dead wood for what we build. We still need 16,000 Euros to complete the project, but our carbon credit

sales should allow us to raise the money we need.

"You should find a way to grow money instead!" my children told me.

We had a good laugh. And then I asked:

"Do you know what people should cultivate in the future?"

They looked off to the right, the way they always do when they're searching for an answer.

"Wheat? ... Corn? ... Coca Cola!"

I smiled while they watched me expectantly.

"Alright, I will tell you. But you must never forget what I am about to say!"

They all nodded in unison.

"People should cultivate un-der-standing! Each person must understand that the planet belongs to us all, and that we have to make sure to respect one another's space in addition to maintaining a genuine awareness of the environment, a "green" consciousness. Inside consciousness lies respect, and this respect guides the ways that humans must behave and evolve.

In our language, we call it *garbawawe*, "right living" or "living harmoniously.'"

And then Walelasoepilemãn, my older son, said:

"That word must not exist in the poachers' language. Because of them, we had to put the ecotourism project on hold."

I nodded. Ecotourism was still a part of our plan for financial autonomy, but as long as the madeireiros were on our land, it was out of the question to bring tourists here.

"Unless the tourists want to spend every hour of their vacation next to bodyguards!" his younger brother, Walelasoekim, said.

We laughed again, but I saw a wave of sadness sweep across my children's faces. I asked them if they remembered the hummingbird nest they found while going to check on the recently planted pupunha crops. My son, Oyexiener, delicately lifted up the palm leaf that the nest was attached to and the baby birds—not much bigger than a half of a thumb—reached their beaks out towards him. He had tears in his eyes, and I chose that moment to tell my children the tale of the hummingbird.

One day, a huge fire swept across the rainforest. All the animals had fled except one hummingbird that kept on and wouldn't stop carrying water in his beak to douse the trees on fire.

"What are you doing, little bird?" an armadillo asked him. *"You can't think that you are going to stop the fire with just the water in your beak!"*

The hummingbird remained focused on his work. "I know very well that I won't stop the fire all by myself, but at least I will have done my part."

Oyexiener was very quiet—which is not at all like him! I remember very clearly the look on his face. I saw that same expression recently when he was choosing his thesis topic for his environmental engineering degree. His mother Adlanes had just called me over to help him choose it.

"No, no," he told her. He cut his mother off with that same expression—"I've already decided to study the effects of deforestation on Suruí land."

I knew then that he, too, would do his part. He is a hummingbird.

With some distance, it is clear to me that teaching my family to love the great rainforest is my biggest and most beautiful accomplishment, along with, of course, having rallied so many people to our cause. We are being asked to share our expertise about the rainforest more and more and I am invited around the world to speak about ways to manage its potential in a sustainable way.

You will never guess who contacted me recently: a company in Abu Dhabi whose representative proposed that we create a rainforest in the middle of the desert of the United Arab Emirates! I found the idea quite surprising but he told me that they have already built a ski slope, so why not a forest? After I consulted with members of our tribe, it was decided that we would ask for 15 million dollars to do this project, in addition to a percentage of the amount generated from ticket sales to visit what the man called "an attraction."

They have not yet answered us, but in the meantime I got another surprise. I was contacted by James Cameron, the director of the movie *Avatar*. He proposed creating a video game with the goal of raising as much awareness as possible about what we are fighting for. I don't know yet if it will come to be, but the money that we could earn from these two propositions would allow us to buy back a part of the land adjacent to our reserve. It used to belong to us—just like all the wood that continues to be stolen from us.

I hope, of course, that the timber poaching will stop one day, I tell my children that there is one thing, in addition to their knowledge, that can never be stolen from them. It is the name of our clan: Gameb.

Gameb refers to the fearsome black wasp. Saying this name aloud will give them their strength.

Saying this name aloud will take you back to what our ancestors taught us, to our ancestors who made us "the true people," raised with a deep respect for their brothers and for the rainforest that nourishes them.

I am able to recover a sense of peace when I say the name of my clan aloud. That name will remind us how it is we are to act in life. And our lives should measure up to what it means: not just as words but as a concrete example that you can refer back to in order to help you lead your people. We must always remember what we are and where we are from if we want to grow in harmony with others and our environment. Gameb is our conscience. We must always act in keeping with it.

I know that my children are proud to carry this name. They are proud of the work we have undertaken to save our forest. I have watched them periodically measure the first tree that we planted together. The small mahogany tree is six meters high as of this writing, and I hope with all my heart that it will one day reach full potential. I hope the same thing for my children. And I hope that we will sing beneath its branches, wishing it a long life for a very long time to come!

AVOIDING AN ETHNO-ENVIRONMENTAL CATASTROPHE

The more than 650 indigenous territories that exist in Brazil today make up the size of the surface area of France, Germany and the Benelux countries combined. Some people would say that this area is only 15% of the surface area of our country. I would counter that these territories have increased in size by 40% since 1987. Moreover, this growth is due to decades of dogged struggle by Indians who knew how to join forces to defend their rights and the rights of Mother Earth.

Currently, at least 150 Indian organizations are fighting to protect the rainforest's threatened biodiversity and its endangered species. Brazil, with its 8.2 million square kilometers (nearly 3.2 million square miles), is home to 10% of the planet's mammals and 13% of its amphibians. The 580 reptiles, 800 amphibians and 3,000 fish make up a wealth that is irreplaceable. Would it not be completely irresponsible to continue sacrificing them at the altar of profits?

Knowing this, our leaders knew how to garner the support of numerous NGOs in Brazil and abroad in order to push the Brazilian government to expand the environmental protection areas and to register indigenous territories in the cadaster (land registry) system that weren't there already.

So, on June 5, 2012, on the occasion of the World Environment Day, President Dilma Rousseff legally recognized seven Indian lands in the states of Amazonas, Acre and Pará, meaning that nearly one million hectares (3,860 square miles) would be protected from then on. This was indeed a good thing; since the beginning of the Growth Acceleration Program during Lula's second term, the surface area of protected territories had sharply

declined. Even though most of the battles for land rights seem to have been won, the struggle against deforestation is far from over. . . .

The figures released by the Brazilian government show that since 2012, after four years of decline, deforestation increased on average by 28%, with spikes as high as 50% in the state of Mato Grosso and even higher in Pará. Izabella Teixeira, the Minister of the Environment, attributed this increase to the lack of enforcement in certain states such as Pará, which has been invaded, she says, by nearly 3,000 clandestine gold and diamond prospectors who act with impunity and clear the land while ignoring cadasters delimiting indigenous lands. Marina Silva, (President Lula's former Minster of the Environment who launched a new party in 2013, the Rede Sustentabilidade) condemned the large-scale collusion between Brasilia and those clearing the land illegally. We Indians think that this increase in deforestation coincides with two other factors: Dilma Rousseff's government expanding the large projects of the Growth Acceleration Program (PAC - Programa de Aceleração do Crescimento) and the forestry code reforms going into effect in 2012.

The forestry code reforms had been more thoroughly enforced during the previous administration of Lula da Silva (2003-2011), which had not served the interests of the ruralistas—the representatives of the farming sector in Parliament. Three years ago, they launched an offensive to relax the code by proposing reforms that not only would pardon any timber poaching occurring before 2008, but that would also never require the landowners to reforest any farms established before this date. This relaxed version of the forestry code reforms was immediately condemned by our leaders and by environmental protection agencies as a major setback that we estimated would lead to a 50% increase in deforestation over the ten years that would follow.

However, under pressure from the powerful agricultural lobby of the ruralistas, President Dilma Rousseff was not able to get the veto that our leaders and all of the ecological groups demanded. In May 2012, the relaxed version of the forestry code was enacted.

The clause in the reform that just about completely pardons the clearing of riverbanks was removed, which is of course good, but the clause demanding the reforestation of the riverbanks as well as the hilltops was not kept. The clause forcing small land owners to preserve 80% of the forest on their land was also significantly relaxed. As for the states

in Amazonia where more than 65% of land is protected (such as the indigenous lands and the Nature Protection Units) the limit of the legal reserve (the legal requirement for landowners to preserve 80% of forests) fell from 80% to 50%. These figures are quite troublesome, but still far too abstract to truly reveal the scope of the catastrophe that they foreshadow.

This 30% difference permitted the annexation of 90,000 hectares (348 square miles) to be used for new infrastructure developed in the framework of large-scale energy projects of PAC.

Consequently, the Floresta Nacional do Tapajós reserve in the state of Pará could be amputated by nearly 30,000 hectares (74,131 acres) for the installation of the hydro-electric power plant Sao Luiz do Tapajós. The Chacorao power plant will require the flooding of a large part of the lands belonging to the Sai Cinza and Munduruku Indians, and one of their sacred sites has already been destroyed in order to build the dam. Additionally, the Santa Isabel power plant will be built in a protected zone of the Serra dos Martírios-Andorinhas Park which neighbors the lands belonging to the Sororo Indians, the Apinayé Indians, the Mãe Maria Indians and the Xamboiá Indians. And I haven't even mentioned the Belo Monte hydroelectric dam in the State of Pará yet . . .

The crown jewel of the eighteen power plants planned in the Amazonian Basin of the Araguaia and the Tocantins rivers is the construction of the Belo Monte plant on the Great Bend of the Xingú River. Construction began in 2011, and it was designed to become the third largest dam in the world, producing 10% of Brazil's electricity needs. For this, 600 square kilometers (231 square miles) of land and part of a nearby national park will be flooded, of which 400 square kilometers (154 square miles) are primary forest. This is an ecological catastrophe that would lead to the expulsion of more than 15,000 Indians, of which the most directly affected will be the Kayapó Indians, the Araweté Indians, the Arara Indians, the Kisêdjê Indians and the Jururna Indians.

Less than 20 km from Belo Monte, still on the Great Bend of the Xingú, the population will also have to confront the arrival of the biggest gold mining company of the region. Led by a branch of the Belo Sun Mining Corporation, open-pit mining will affect once more the Arara and Juruna Indian lands but also the land of the Xikrin and Trincheira Bacajá Indians. One of the main problems that come with it is the cyanide

extraction process, whose environmental impact is simply unimaginable. Another problem is that 80% of the flow of this part of the Xingú River will be reduced. As many as 600 species of fish were identified in this river. Do I need to add that certain species only live and reproduce there? Reducing the Xingú River to this extent will lead to the extinction of most of these species, and will consequently deprive indigenous populations of their primary source of food.

The Brazilian Constitution of 1988 and the United Nations Declaration on the Rights of Indigenous Peoples, however, stipulate that indigenous peoples, whose lands could be affected by these kinds of projects, be consulted first. But they were not, even despite a report from the FUNAI in 2009 establishing that the lack of fish resulting from these projects would necessitate the displacement of these groups. The presence of a dozen groups of Indians in voluntary isolation near the dam sites and the mine sites was not taken into account either. Not a single precautionary measure was taken on their behalf.

Many social movements, environmental activists, and Indian leaders directly affected by this (including the Kayapó chief Raoni Metuktire and his successor Meagron Txucarramãe) vehemently condemned the lack of studies evaluating the environmental impact and the absence of consultation with the native populations. These groups were able to get the license for the plant suspended for non-compliance with the Constitution of Brazil as well as with their right to free, prior, and informed consent established at Convention No. 169 of the International Labor Organization. But the federal supreme court intervened, saying that any delays regarding the construction site would threaten the national economy.

The construction started up again.

In 2011, an arbitration of the Inter-American Commission on Human Rights triggered the suspension of construction as long as the indigenous populations remained unconsulted and there was no protection of isolated groups. The government reacted by denying all illegal actions against the rights and protection of the communities concerned. It also threated to retract its financial contribution to the Organization of American States.

The construction began again.

Chief Raoni and Antonia Melo da Silva, activist and spokesperson for the Xingú Vivo Para Sempre movement (uniting the residents and the indigenous peoples for the

Xingú River basin) organized rallies in several Brazilian cities as well as in New York, Rome, and Paris to protest the continuation of the construction site and the dam projects on the Tapajós and Teles Pires Rivers.

In March of 2011, I gave a press conference in the Latin American House in Paris with Sheyla Yakarepi Juruna, the representative of the Juruna people in the basin of the Xingú River, as well as Ruth Buendia Mestoquiari, the president of the Asháninka people who live near the Ene River in Peru. We denounced the catastrophic impact of the dams as well as the impact of the involvement of businesses like GDF and Alstom on the environment.

In 2013, once again in Paris, the activists responded to the call from Planète Amazone and the citizen initiative End Ecocide in Europe and got the support of more than 20 French and European parliamentarians, as well as the support of Christine Taubira, the French garde des Sceaux (similar to the U.S. Attorney General). In Brazil, angry indigenous populations occupied the Belo Monte construction site for several weeks to ensure that indigenous peoples are consulted and provided with an analysis of the ethno-environmental consequences of building the dam. They got the support of numerous environmental organizations such as Planete Amazone, Amazone Watch, Survival International, Greenpeace Brazil, Força e Coragem, INCRA, Aquaverde, and the Idle No More, Gota d'Água and Xingú Vivo Para Sempre movements, as well as the Paroles de Nature and the mass demonstrations of Stop Belo Monte. I have probably left some out, but even so, petitions with more than a million signatures were also submitted, and were supported by such French and American celebrities as Vincent Cassel, Agnès Soral, Hugues Aufray, Abd Al Malik, Pierre Richard, Nicolas Hulot, Jacques Weber, Marion Cotillard, Rémi Gaillard, James Cameron, Sigourney Weaver and Arnold Schwarzenegger.

Confronted with this pressure from the international community, the government said it was willing to expand the dialogue but not willing to stop the construction, since "too many investments had already been made." Izabella Teixeira still maintains that the recent surge in deforestation is not linked to the enormous construction projects despite studies showing that the main targets of deforestation are at these construction sites. The Brazilian Energy Expansion Plan has scheduled 30 new dams to be built between

the time of this writing and 2020, in other words, three per year. As for the Belo Monte construction company, Norte Energia, it proposed relocating the Indians whose lands will be flooded to the peripheral areas of Altamira.

Yet, with the arrival of 15,000 workers to the project site, the town saw its population triple in ten years. Since no infrastructure had been provided to offset such growth, the town now faces an upsurge in violence: drug trafficking, rape, prostitution, illegal weapons possession, and violent attacks. I ask you: is forcing the native people to be relocated into this suburb where violence is the norm an acceptable form of compensation?

If we use what happened here in Rondônia as an example, then no. It is well known that the people expelled prior to the construction of the dams in Santo Antônio and Jirau near Porto Velho were actually relocated to colonies of grim huts in Vila Mutum, the boomtown that emerged to house the 25,000 workers sent to work on the dams. This city has been eroded by violence and prostitution, shaken by social upheavals caused by working conditions, and has not provided a favorable environment to these displaced populations. These people are unable to live off of the river's resources as they used to since it is now dried out and polluted. Their lives have been completely broken by relocation.

GDF Suez, builder and majority shareholder of the Jirau dam, may have indeed reminded everyone that the dam is the first project of its size to have obtained the new "green" Hydropower Sustainability Assessment Protocol certification (a certification put in place by the global dam industry). GDF Suez may have indeed shown off the $600 million that they invested into the variety of corporate social responsibility programs and environmental offsets that come along with their projects. But it is my opinion that the Jirau dam and the Madeira River complex have, at this point, generated more tension than electricity.

Worst of all is that the Jirau dam, whose completion is slated for 2015, is heralded as a CDP (Clean Development Mechanism) project (one presenting a way to earn carbon credits). Proponents of the dams say they would actually generate clean electricity, preventing Brazil from having to build coal-fired or gas-fired power plants, both major emitters of carbon dioxide. This has justified the subsidies and other privileges granted to these big projects by the Brazilian government and international institutions. But much recent research has refuted these arguments by showing that the dams are in fact significant contributors of methane in the atmosphere, a gas formed by the decomposition

of vegetation that has been submerged as a result of these projects. Emitting carbon dioxide is bad enough—methane emissions are twenty times worse!

DECREE 303

I will now ask you to commit two dates to memory that mark a dramatic turning point in the history of Amazonia and the rights of its indigenous peoples.

On March 21, 2012, the Constitution and Justice Commission of the Chamber of Deputies (the lower house of the Brazilian National Congress) confirmed the eligibility of a new amendment to the constitution proposed by the ruralistas which would transfer responsibility of the land registry of indigenous land and zones of environmental protection to the National Congress. If approved, the validity of registered indigenous lands like our own will be challenged. Additionally, any future requests to the FUNAI to delimit indigenous lands will be screened by the government. If requests are deemed incompatible with the goals of the Growth Acceleration Program, they could then be overridden.

And that's not all.

In the wake of these propositions, Dilma Rousseff signed Decree 303 on July 16, 2012, which is important to mention since it threatens our accomplishments and our constitutional rights by subjecting our territories to the extraction of raw materials, to unregulated circulation of people, and to the construction of dams and the roads required to reach them. Here are a few of the most unsettling excerpts:

—*The ownership of rivers and lakes located on indigenous land may be reconsidered if they become a question of public interest.*

—*Indigenous lands do not include research and extraction of mining resources that will depend still on the authorization from National Congress.*

—*Indigenous land may not get in the way of any interests of national defense including the installation of military bases, units, and posts and other interventions, expansion of road networks, and strategic extraction of energy resources.*

This decree will also give more legal protection to non-Indian land owners who will be permitted to expand their ownership over previously registered land. Additionally, non-Indian land owners will no longer need to turn over the land they currently occupy ...

EPILOGUE

November 6, 2013
10:05 am
7th of September Reserve

My bodyguard slid the USB drive into a pocket of his cargo pants.

"I'll take it to your children. You can count on me."

A raindrop fell onto his nose. He jerked his head back.

"At least you have your cocar to keep your nose dry!" He smiled and wiped the rain off his face.

I touched the feathers of the chief's cocar crowning my head. This one had been my father's favorite.

"I will give you one, if you like."

He burst out laughing.

"Although it would go really well with my military getup, I doubt my boss would go for it!"

I laughed with him and made him promise to at least try one on.

"Ok!" he finally said. "But now it's time to find some shelter, isn't it?"

I looked at the big pacohb to our right. Its leaves were perfectly still despite the presence of four blue macaws perched in its highest branches. I motioned for Sergente to look up at them. Because of the pesticide spraying, the poaching, and the destruction of their natural habitat, they had become a rare sight.

"These macaws are part of the 627 endangered animal species in Brazil. This number has tripled in 15 years . . ."

Sergente was listening closely so I added that these species were listed in the Brazilian

Red List of Endangered Species, the official document compiled by Carlos Minc, our Environment Minister. Within its pages are 69 mammals, 160 birds, 20 reptiles, 16 amphibians, 154 fish and 208 invertebrates.

"This is the first time I have ever seen these macaws in the wild," Sergente said, his eyes trained on their bright blue feathers. "They're so big!"

"About 70cm," I added, listening attentively to their loud squawking. (70 cm is nearly 28 inches.) "The rain is not ready to fall yet," I announced. "We have a lull."

Sergente cocked his head towards the macaws.

"Are you telling me they told you that?"

I smiled and told him it was time for me to tell him the story of the pacohb tree in which the birds had been screeching so joyfully.

In the past, the Paiter Suruí people were made up of at least 10 clans. Unfortunately, they fought a lot amongst themselves. One day, one of the clans declared war on the Gameb clan. Right before arriving at the Gameb village, the chief brought his warriors together around the white trunk of this giant pacohb tree to check their bows, count their arrows and prepare their attack. As he opened his mouth to give his men his final instructions, the pacohb tree started to speak. The tree asked: "My children, where are you going?" Blinded by thirst for vengeance and not knowing how to answer, the chief ignored the pacohb. But when the warriors finally arrived at the Gameb village, they were all killed.

"All of them?" Sergente exclaimed. "How's that possible?"

"The story doesn't say, but I can't help but compare the chief's behavior to how our leaders are acting now: they are blinded by their thirst for profit. Assuming that the trees still want to speak to them, what would they do if while walking one day this pacohb tree asked them the same question: 'My children, where are you going?' Would they have the wisdom to try to answer the question? Would they be wise enough to realize that they are bringing about our own demise?"

The blue macaws flew away, rustling the leaves of the giant tree. I watched as they flew farther and farther away. What startled them? The answer I was dreading came in on a breeze.

"Chainsaws," I said, looking at Sergente.

He put one hand to the strap of his gun and motioned for me to walk in front of him. I sighed and obeyed. Even today, forty trucks of freshly cut trunks would leave our land. I couldn't stop these lists of numbers from rattling around my brain. They had no way out.

The CODEMA, an environmental department of the FUNAI created in 1989, admitted that 85% of indigenous lands, despite being officially demarcated, were still being invaded by illegal logging and mining companies. 150 territories were affected by railway lines, 54 by timber cutting, 28 by mining, in addition to the 120 that suffered from or would suffer from the indirect effects associated with electric power work and with the expansion of the road network allowing access to hydroelectric infrastructure. GITPA (International Work Group for Political Affairs) condemned the fact that the PAC (Growth Acceleration Program) and the forestry code reforms had set us back more than 40 years in terms of social and environmental rights: "We're back to the ideology of the 1970s when the military government was building the Transamazonian Highway under the slogan 'Security and Development.'" Since then, nearly one fifth of the Amazon rainforest has disappeared. And a soccer-field-sized area of land would go up in smoke every two seconds.

"How much longer will we need to sound the alarm?" I asked Sergente, still following close on my heels. "Why haven't they heeded the warnings from scientists? We know that when trees are burned, or cut down—or they rot—the carbon that they contain is returned back into the atmosphere—which is not a bad thing on a small scale. But recent studies published in the scientific journal Nature show that deforestation and human activity in the Amazon rainforest—already responsible for 20% of global greenhouse gasses—is on the verge of becoming a net-emitter of CO_2.

"Wait," Sergente said, "you're saying the Amazon rainforest, our very own beautiful Mother Earth, provider of so much ingenuity, contributes to global warming?" His voice caught in his throat. "How could we, children of the rainforest, have let this happen?"

I couldn't bring myself to respond.

"Explain it, Almir." Sergente seemed worried. He hesitated, and then began. "Have we already gone past the point of no return? Is it too late to save the planet?"

I shrugged.

"The planet is very sick, that's for certain, but the impact of humans, despite all of our arrogance, only goes down a few dozen kilometers into the earth's surface, whose radius

is 6,000km (about 373 miles). So, we have no real way of 'saving the planet,' since it will most certainly outlive us. That being said, we are currently destroying the equilibrium that made the earth a system where life, trees, and flowers were able to develop."

I shook my head and lowered my eyes.

"It's that equilibrium that we should be trying to save. The pressure we put on the existing ecosystems to satisfy our needs has never been as intense as it is now. The decrease in biodiversity we are observing today is unprecedented."

"So is it too late?"

I shrugged again.

"Time will tell if our stupidity is irreparable, but the only way to avoid this situation from ending badly for our children and for their children is to act now and do our part."

"You're always saying that, but what can I do, concretely?"

I stopped walking.

"It seems essential that we become responsible consumers who are conscious of what we are doing. Did you know that today, 86% of the world's population lives in countries that demand more of Nature than what their ecosystems can renew?

"No..."

"And according to the Global Footprint Network, the international think tank measuring the amount of natural resources that we need, in 2050 we will need the equivalent of the resources from two planets to meet the need of what we are consuming!"

"Two planets? Well, what are we going to do?"

"There are solutions being put into place, like making a massive transition to renewable energy sources, rethinking urbanization, mobility and taxation, and recycling more. But these solutions must become a priority for the whole planet."

"So what can I do at my level?"

"Do you eat a lot of meat?"

"Uh ... yes. Why?"

"Well, meat production emits 20-30% more greenhouse gasses than growing vegetables..."

"You're not asking me to become a vegetarian, are you?"

"No, but you should question your consumption habits and rethink the ones that aren't compatible with a sustainable future."

"Okay . . ."

"You could also choose products that you're sure come from sustainably managed sources."

"Okay. . ."

"You could also support the efforts of NGOs to lobby the government and use your new experience as a conscientious consumer to make as many people as possible aware of what's at stake."

"Okay . . ."

"And you could use as a model the only engineer that's capable of creating a production cycle without consuming fossil fuels or producing waste."

Sergente frowned.

"Do I know him?"

"Of course, you do. And all of the engineer's ideas are here, right in front of you, free of charge!"

"Oh yes, of course; Mother Nature!"

"Exactly. Nature has already solved most of the problems we are being faced with right now. Sometimes it took thousands of years to do it, but the solutions are there. Isn't that yet another priceless gift?"

"Of course," Sergente answered, surveying the nature surrounding us. "But can you give me an example? I don't really see how by observing these mosquitoes here I will be able to find a solution to anything."

"Scientists asked themselves the very same question."

"They did?"

"They first observed what you know already, that a mosquito bite is painless. Next, they thought that by copying the conical shape of its proboscis they could create medical needles that we would feel less than the ones we were using at the time. Today millions of those needles are sold. And everyone benefits from them. I could also give you the example of the tiny robots inspired by bees that might soon be able to map out our territory."

"Bee robots?!"

"Harvard researchers are planning to reproduce the collaborative behavior of a bee swarm and have each one of these 'bee robots' collect data that could then be transmit-

ted among them. The researchers would then be able to divide the tasks of tracking, exploration and mapping among the groups of bees, like in a real colony. They'd have what they need to carry out missions in difficult-to-access places, like some regions of our territory, or to live-monitor any deforestation happening, or even to seed crops . . ."

"I must admit that is pretty practical, but I am not really looking forward to coming across swarms of bee robots. . . ."

"Granted! But then there's also termite mounds. Architects like Mick Pearce have realized that the design of such habitats makes it possible to maintain a nearly constant temperature, completely independent of external changes in temperature. So, he got the idea from this architectural design to create buildings with passive air-conditioning that are capable of absorbing heat during the day and restoring it at night.

"Not bad!"

"I could also give you the example of how people have been studying the eyes of flies to help blind people, the diving suit inspired by shark skin, or even the development of a used water treatment cycle without chemicals or waste. All of these projects have come about since the late 1990s from observations of natural phenomena. They are all a part of a specific scientific field called biomimicry."

"But from what you've taught me, you Indians have been practicing biomimicry for much longer than that, right? Haven't you always tried solving your problems by observing how Nature does it?"

"Yes, and that's why we are committed to sharing the entirety of what we have learned with everyone else. I can't stress enough how important observing nature is for creating a sustainable future."

Sergente was quiet for a few moments.

"Okay, but besides depriving me of meat and telling me to live like a termite, don't you have anything quicker?"

I answered in the most serious tone I could manage. "We cannot change the world in a few days' time. And it's better that way, isn't it?"

Sergente arched his eyebrows. I grinned.

"Just remember that any lasting change must be done over time."

"So, you are not a proponent of strong-arm tactics, then?"

"Violence is sometimes necessary, but we Suruí have always managed to avoid it.

The price one pays involves far too many heavy consequences."

"I know."

"Have you ever tried riding a unicycle?"

"If you're talking about a bike with only one wheel, then no, I have never really had the inclination!"

"Well in my opinion, engaging in a struggle like ours is a little like riding a unicycle. If you pedal too slowly you will fall backwards, if you pedal too quickly you will fall forward. To stay upright and reach your goal you have to operate using a delicate balance between strength and gentleness, firmness and flexibility, between going forward and going back—exactly how I'm trying to lead our fight to save the rainforest."

"I see. But what about you? What will you do to 'play your part?'"

"I have to convince our leaders to put governmental regulations in place that are based on our model for sustainable rainforest management."

The sound of chainsaws suddenly split our ears. Sergente motioned me to keep walking.

"Hurry up, or your enemies won't let you live to see those laws put in place!"

I stepped forward.

"I want to tell our leaders that Brazil has a strength that it has ignored for a long time. And that strength is indigenous knowledge!"

The sound of my voice suddenly competed with the sound of a sinister cracking of a falling tree in the distance. I winced. The clicking of Sergente's gun and the sound of his breathing reminded me that we had to keep moving. Faster. I wanted to believe that his heavy breathing was out of exertion, not out of fear. Should I ask him? No. Our warriors never admit they are afraid of being killed. Or that they are afraid of killing, Marimop would say. Keeping that secret to themselves was the bulwark of their human dignity. The right to continue to be heroes in the memory of their people.

I kept walking. I realized that my heart was beating normally. Why was I so calm? I turned back to Sergente. He was on the lookout, gripping his gun.

"The madeireiros are too busy cutting down our trees to come and get me," I said, trying to reassure him.

"It's my job to doubt that you're right. We have to hurry up."

I walked more quickly, still as calm as before. Maybe I had simply accepted the

likelihood of being assassinated. I shook my head, calling myself a fool. But why else would I be so calm on a gut level? Maybe as a way of girding myself against the claws of fear. I kept walking, still searching for a satisfying answer.

The fear showed up when we passed the first house of our village. I had probably pushed this fear to the very farthest edges of my mind, like how the eye of a hurricane is always still—a hurricane that would end up destroying me. I shook my head, perhaps to chase away this thought. I caught sight of my mother, sitting barefoot near the doorway of her house. She was wearing a black dress with red, yellow, and blue flowers on it. She was concentrating on the tucumã nuts she was breaking on the stump in front of her. Soon a new necklace would be born of her quick, precise, beautiful artistry. Her gestures making those necklaces told the story of everything she was able to create in her life. I gripped the two necklaces that I wore around my neck. Their soft, supple texture helped me set aside the strong emotions that had taken hold of me.

Pow-pow-pow-pow-pow. The sound behind me made me jump.

"Everything's all right," Sergente called from behind me. "It's your son!"

I burst out laughing when I saw Oyexiener roll up to us riding a red Honda 125 motor bike.

"I finally got it working, dad!"

He wore a cocar of gray feathers around his head, like the two boys at his side. Dark blue ritual body paintings decorated their arms, legs and chests. I wanted to pick them up and hug them close to me but instead I watched as Oyexiener rolled our way.

"Did you see, Bà? I fixed it! This will help us watch over our territory."

"Sure it will, but I'm not sure that Bermuda shorts and flip flops are the ideal outfit for chasing off madeireiros." He looked at his feet.

"I know, dad, but this is my mechanic's outfit!"

My mother called out to us in her deep voice from the doorway of the house.

"Get off of that thing right now, Oyexiener, you are going to hurt yourself!"

He smiled at me slyly.

"Hey, Grandma!" he called to her, "do you want to take a ride?"

"You must be trying to send me to Gorakoy, you silly boy! I will never ever get on that smelly thing!"

He rode over to her, laughing. I watched them tease each other and I was suddenly moved. Marimop and my mother often teased each other like this. I heard Sergente clear his throat so I turned to him.

"Everything looks okay here, right?" I asked.

He nodded and smiled. Since the mood had lightened a bit, I decided to tell him one thing that was still weighing on my mind.

"I think that we will be able to invent a sustainable model for our planet when we can combine our knowledge with and create connections between the many other models that already exist in the world, don't you agree? We alone can respond in an adequate way to the question that the pacohb tree asks us: 'Where are you going, my children?'"

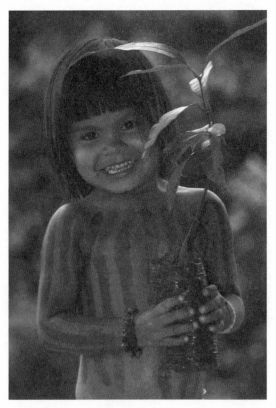

Laetitia Suruí was six when she became a symbol of reforestation.
T. Pizer, Aquaverde

Almir and his wife Ivaneide during the Human Rights Award ceremony in Geneva in December 2008.
Magali Girardin, Aquaverde

AFTERWORD

BY CORINE SOMBRUN

On March 8, 2013, Almir Narayamoga Suruí was conferred an honorary doctorate by Unir, the Federal University of Rondônia. The president of the university, Maria Berenice Alho da Costa Tourinho reiterated that "a public university must take into account the commitment of the recipient, both past and present, to causes that ennoble humanity. This status also expresses the desire of the Unir to salute and support the campaign of all the indigenous peoples of Rondônia." Almir took the stage to thank the president and the other professors of the geography department. "I am honored by this historical tribute to Rondônia," he said. "I dedicate this recognition to my mother and to all the members of my family who educated me and supported me in my fight for sustainable development and my fight for human rights."

On April 10, 2013, the United Nations Forum on Forests met in Istanbul for their 10th session. Almir Narayamoga Suruí was awarded the Forest Heroes Award along with four other individuals. Jan McAlpine, the Director of the UN Forum on Forests Secretariat, stressed that the laureates are remarkable people. "Thanks to them, it is clear that there exist creative ways to demonstrate that we are an integral part of the rainforests, and that the rainforests are also a part of us. Their stories are sources of inspiration and they are our models."

On December 12, 2013, at the World Forum of Human Rights at the Centro International de Convencoes do Brasil (International Convention Center of Brazil) in Brasilia, the Brazil's president at the time, Dilma Rousseff, and the Human Rights Minister Maria do Rosario, head of the Secretariat of the Presidency of the Republic

for Human Rights, awarded the Human Rights Prize to Almir Narayamoga Suruí. This award marks the highest honor of the Brazilian government and is given to individuals or institutions that have completed important work in the field of Human Rights. The criteria for the award include historical accomplishments, development of relevant actions, and the implementation of innovative practices related to human rights.

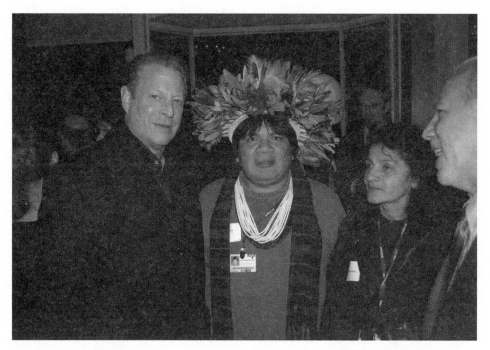

Almir with Al Gore during the 2009 Copenhagen Climate Change conference.
(Associação Metareilá Suruí)

ACKNOWLEDGMENTS

I particularly want to thank Agnès Soral, Thomas Pizer, Luiza Corrêa Pizer and Serge Sandor, who helped me to meet the great Almir Narayamoga and the Surui tribe and to the Amazon forest as I have never seen it before.

—*Corine Sombrun*

PUBLISHER'S NOTE

For their assistance in making the translation possible and for their support, we would like to thank Julia Grawemeyer, François-Olivier Chené, Thomas Pizer, Sean Murphy, Jennifer Powers, James Kiehle, David Ter-Avanesyan, Craig Stennet, Corine Sombrun, Aquaverde, Associação Metareilá Suruí, Alice Tassel, Brigitte Perivier, and Valentine Schaffner. Special thanks go to Chief Almir Narayamoga Suruí and the Paiter Suruí for their powerful message that has been our honor to publish in this english translation.

—*TS*

PUBLISHER'S UPDATE

CAMPAIGN FOR THE PROTECTION OF THE SURUÍ PEOPLE AND PRESERVATION OF THEIR NATIVE LAND IN THE AMAZON RAINFOREST AS OF OCTOBER 2016:

Below is an extract of the "Cry for Help," dated 13th October 2016, received from Almir Narayamoga Suruí, Chief of the Paiter Suruí people:

• *Massive illegal and mafia-driven invasion*
"Since the beginning of this year 2016, we are suffering a total invasion of illegal loggers and miners of diamonds and gold. Every day, over 300 trucks leave our territory filled with wood, which represents 600 hectares of deforested forests. And it continues to increase, whilst according to the Constitution of Brazil, it is illegal to deforest an indigenous reservation. On the ground, the illegal loggers have heavy means, with Caterpillar machines. We have found mercury and cyanide in 3 rivers of Suruí territory because of the miners!"

• *Danger to our families*
"The implications are disastrous. In addition to environmental damage and the challenge to our way of life, this invasion directly endangers our families and our children. Indeed, we are under the threat of weapons of loggers and miners! Either one collaborates, or they put a gun to our heads! In addition, they try to bribe some of my people with money. For fear and lack of alternatives, some of my people accept against their first resolve to protect the forest. The situation is terrible!"

• *Lack of action from the current Brazilian government*
"Despite our appeals for help against this mafia, the new government did not react. By its silence, it is [a] silent accomplice of this destruction of the forest and the endangering of our people!"

• *Cry for help*
"We don't know what to do anymore, HELP!"

<div align="right">Almir Narayamoga Suruí</div>

CHIEF ALMIR NARAYAMOGA SURUÍ, chieftain of the Paiter Suruí people of the Rondônia region of Brazil, has been a leader in the fight to save the earth's largest remaining rainforests, and has utilized modern technology to further this crusade. In developing a carbon deficit formula for his tribal lands and those of other neighboring tribes, he has created a system whereby the reforestation and preservation of the "lung of the Earth" are of greater financial worth than their destruction. Now, three years after the original publication of this book, he and his family and tribe continue to wage this battle against great odds for the environment and human rights, not only for Amazonian tribes, but for all indigenous people around the world.

CORINE SOMBRUN is the author of several books, including *Journal of A Shaman's Apprentice* (2002) *In the Footsteps of Geronimo* (2008), and *Spirits of the Steppe: With the Last Shamans of Mongolia* (2012). Born in Burkino Faso, Africa, in 1961, she studied music and musicology in Montreal, and while on assignment for the BBC World Service in 2001 in Mongolia was identified as a shaman herself by a Mongol shaman. A world traveler and lecturer, she has appeared on Ted Talks and furthers her studies on the corollary between shamanistic practice and neurological science.

JULIA GRAWEMEYER is professor of French language, literature and culture at Denison College in Ohio, and has translated fiction, film and critical essays. *Save the Planet* is her first translation of a published full length book.

Back cover photo: Kennedy, Mopiri Suruí's son, also called "Piti Chief," decided at age 4 that he would devote himself to protecting his ancestors' forest. © *Thomas Pizer, Aquaverde*